AN IN-DEPTH STUDY OF
THE BOOK OF JOB

AND THE LORD *Blessed* JOB

Elizabeth Bagwell Ficken

Printed in the United States of America
First Printing, 2016
W & E Publishing, Cary, NC

Cover: Jeannine Klingbeil

ISBN-10: 0990593304
ISBN-13: 978-0990593300

Special thanks to:
my husband Wade for going through the trials of life with me,
my family and friends for their encouragement while I was writing this study,
and Linda Walters and Christen Merithew for proofreading my rough drafts.

God's voice thunders in marvelous ways;
He does great things beyond our understanding.
Job 37:5 [NIV]

Free videos, handouts, leader's guides, and podcasts
are available as supplemental resources for this study.
Go to elizabethficken.com for more information.

TABLE OF CONTENTS

	Introduction		7
	My Bible Story		8
	Do you know Jesus?		9
	Helpful Hints		10
	Lessons:		
1.	Who is Job?	Job 1:11-2:12	13
2.	The Greatest of All People	Job 1:2-5	17
3.	Who is Satan?	Job 1:6-12	19
4.	The End of Life as He Knew It	Job 1:13-22	22
5.	Satan Strikes Again	Job 2:1-9	26
6.	Maintaining Integrity	Job 2:10-13	30
7.	The Big View and the Black View	Overview and Job 3	33
8.	And Now a Word from His Friend	Job 4 and 5	38
9.	Discouragement, Defensiveness, and More Death Wishes	Job 6 and 7	42
10.	Short but Not Sweet	Job 8	47
11.	It's Complicated	Job 9 and 10	51
12.	Zophar Speaks	Job 11	55
13.	Wisdom, Integrity, and Hope	Job 12, 13, and 14	59
14.	What He Would Say to God	Job 14	62
15.	Words from the Oh-So Wise Eliphaz	Job 15	67
16.	The Anchor in the Storm	Job 16 and 17	72
17.	The Anchor in the Storm: Part Two	Job 16 and 17	76
18.	Expecting Death	Job 18 and 19	79
19.	Zophar Attacks!	Job 20	85
20.	They Live Long and Prosper	Job 21	89
21.	Eloquent Condemnation from Eliphaz	Job 22	92
22.	Job's Eloquent Answer to Eliphaz	Job 23 and 24	97
23.	Bildad Tries to Be Wise	Job 25 and 26	101
24.	Job's Resolution of Righteousness	Job 27	106
25.	Where is Wisdom?	Job 28	110
26.	Then and Now	Job 29 and 30	112
27.	Job's Closing Argument	Job 31	116
28.	Whose Turn Is It Now?	Job 32 and 33	119

29. The Best Defense	Job 34 and 35	123
30. Elihu's Zeal for the Lord	Job 36 and 37	129
31. God Speaks	Job 38, 39, 40 and 41	135
32. The Lord Asks Job	Job 38	138
33. God's Wisdom Over His Wild Kingdom	Job 38:39-40:2	143
34. Convicting Questions	Job 40:1-14	147
35. The Monster in the Marsh	Job 40:15-24	152
36. A Creature Under God's Control	Job 41	156
37. Job Responds	Job 42:1-6	160
38. The Rest of the Story	Job 42:7-10	164
39. P.S. Job Was Blessed	Job 42:10-17	167
40. Remembering and Reflecting	The Book of Job	172

Endnotes	178
Suggested Resources	182
Prayer Requests and Blessings	184
Notes	206
Other In-depth Bible Studies by Elizabeth Bagwell Ficken	212
Information on free resources at elizabethficken.com	214

INTRODUCTION

Dear Friend,

I'm looking forward to studying the book of Job with you. This book of the Bible has been of great interest to me for years. The truths it contains regarding the wisdom and sovereignty and power of the Lord are foundational for life on Earth. The perspectives on suffering discussed in the dialogues between Job and his friends are as relevant today as they were thousands of years ago. The concepts of blamelessness, righteousness, faith and fearing the Lord shine through the difficult circumstances. And as you can tell from the title of the study, the blessing of the Lord upon Job is important to recognize. I hope you will come to understand that the Lord's blessings come in a variety of ways—and they don't always come in the ways that we would expect them.

Disaster. Death. Pain. Suffering. Grief. These are the undeniable extremes that we will encounter in the book of Job. These are some of the serious experiences that we must reflect on and even enter into as we study this book of Scripture. There will be no sugar-coating of the tragedy and trauma that Job endures. So, I'm just preparing you right from the start. This will not be a light-hearted, easy stroll through the park on a sunny day.

But we already know the end of the story. And we will keep the end of the story in mind as we trudge through the very difficult thoughts and questions and conversations between Job and his friends.

At the beginning and middle and end of this tragedy is the triumph of God.

Disaster happens. Despair rises. Disenchantment takes over.

But before, during, and after all of this . . . God Almighty, the Creator of Heaven and Earth reigns supreme. His character, His nature, His wisdom, and His ways are above and beyond everything any man or any creature can fathom.

In response to all of Job's comments, and in response to all of his friends' perspectives, the Lord God declares the truth that Job must realize, accept, submit to, surrender to, repent, believe and rest in: God is God.

Knowing Him is the greatest blessing of all.

I am so thankful that my life, and everything that happens in my life, is in the hands of the One Who is perfect in wisdom and faithful in love. Our Lord God can be trusted and He is worthy of worship. Please join me now as we learn to recognize the blessings of the Lord and train ourselves to bless His Name at all times.

MY BIBLE STORY

I love my Bible! But I have about 15 of them on my bookshelf, including a Hebrew and a Greek translation, so which one do I love to use for reading and studying? I'd like to answer that question with my Bible story.

The earliest Bible that I remember reading was a children's New Testament Living Bible. It was a birthday present from a friend when I was eight years old! I tried to read the book of Revelation but didn't get very far.

The next Bible that I received was a King James Version from my parents and it was my church Bible. I don't remember reading it, but I must have taken it to Sunday School with me because I found a Psalm 23 bookmark in it. That was the first well-known Scripture to me.

When I was fourteen I began using a Bible which my father felt was an excellent translation. The New English Bible is not very well known, but it was the Bible that made me begin to know God's Word, especially the letter to the Ephesians. I underlined verses and took it to Bible studies in high school.

My first Bible with cross-references and helpful notes was the Ryrie Study Bible in the King James Version. I bought it after high school graduation and used it for my quiet times and Bible study and sermon notes for about 10 years—through college and early marriage and the births of my children! It was falling apart and the bookbinder recommended a durable covering: blue canvas. I call it my blue jean Bible now!

Then I became aware of the New King James Version and decided it would be nice to leave behind Thee's and Thou's of the Old King James… so I bought The Woman's Study Bible NJKV. It was refreshing to read God's truths in a new translation in a Bible that had clean pages on which for me to make new notes. Familiar verses were lovely and overlooked verses began to stand out as they had not before. The changing of Bible translations became a new adventure for me.

I have read through the Bible in the NIV, NLT, NET, NAS, NKJ, ESV, HCSB and The Complete Jewish Bible. It's description states: "Easily see how the Old Testament points to Jesus and quickly get a handle on all major Jewish customs! Enjoy seeing Hebrew keywords. Easily get a handle on the Jewish roots of Christianity!" An excellent new translation that I am enjoying is the LSB (Legacy Standard Bible); it's an update to the NAS. The LSB Scripture journals are wonderful for taking extra notes.

I've received precious Bibles as gifts as an adult, including a friend's German Bible, my grandmother's 100-year-old-Bible that my mother remembered from her childhood, and one that I call my "coloring Bible" which allows me to meditate on, color and delight in Scriptures which have been illustrated.

Jesus loves me this I know, for my Bible tells me so! I love God's Word and I love my Bible—whichever one I may be reading at any given time.

DO YOU KNOW JESUS?

This is the most important question in this study. Please notice that I didn't ask you if you know about Jesus. But do you know Him, personally?

The Bible teaches that God loves you.
"For God so loved the world . . . that He gave His one and only son that whoever believes in Him will not perish, but have eternal life." John 3:16 ESV

And it teaches that God wants you to know Him personally.
"Now this is eternal life, that men may know Him, the only true God, and Jesus Christ whom He has sent." John 17:3 ESV

But . . . people are separated from God by their sin.
"Your sinful acts have alienated you from your God" Isaiah 59:2 NET

Sin causes us to miss the very best for our life.
"Jesus said, 'I came that you might have life and have it to the full." John 10:10 NIV

Sin causes us to face death and judgment.
"The wages of sin is death." Romans 3:32 NAS
"Those who do not know God . . . will pay the penalty of eternal destruction away from the presence of the Lord." 2 Thessalonians 1:8-9 NAS

But there is a solution! Jesus Christ died and conquered death for you! We deserve death and judgment, but Jesus took upon Himself the punishment for our sins, so that we could have a personal relationship with God.
"For there is only one God and one Mediator who can reconcile God and humanity-- the man Christ Jesus. He gave his life to purchase freedom for everyone." 1 Timothy 2:5-6 NLT

It's not enough just to know this. Each of us by faith must receive Jesus Christ if we want to know God personally.
"To all who have received Him—those who believe in His name—He has given the right to become God's children." John 1:12 NET
"For it is by grace you have been saved, through faith—and this not from yourselves, it is the gift of God." Ephesians 2:8 NIV

The ABC's of faith involve:
<u>Acknowledging your need</u>—admitting you have sinned and desiring to turn from sin. (1 John 1:8-9)
<u>Believing Jesus Christ died in your place</u> and rose again to be your Savior—providing forgiveness for your sins. (1 Corinthians 15:3-4:17)
<u>Choosing to invite Christ</u> to direct your life. (Romans 10:9)

Your desire to have a personal relationship with God can be expressed through a simple prayer like this:
"Dear Lord, I want to know You personally. Thank you for sending Jesus who died in my place and rose again to be my Savior. Please forgive my sins. I am willing, with your help, to turn from my sins. Come into my life and lead me. Amen."

For illustrations and more information, go to **SONLIFE.COM** resources

HELPFUL HINTS

If you are new to in-depth Bible study. You will need a Bible. Please feel free to use the version of your choice. There are many translations. If you are using a Catholic Bible or a Jewish Old Testament it will be helpful for you to also use a modern version of the Bible which includes the Old and New Testament.

I recommend the following versions which are available for free at online Bible study websites, in smartphone and tablet apps (see recommendations on the next page), or for purchase in Christian bookstores. They are usually referred to by the letters in parentheses.

New King James Version (NKJV)	New American Standard Version (NASB)
New International Version (NIV)	Holman Christian Standard Bible (HCSB)
English Standard Version (ESV)	Legacy Standard Bible (LSB)

This study was written using multiple translations. I have found that I can gain understanding of the meaning of verses by reading other versions of the same passage. Two other popular Bibles are *The Message* and the New Living Translation (NLT); these are both wonderful versions for comparative reading, but are not as appropriate for in-depth study.

Planning time for your lesson. Set aside a specific amount of time to work on the lesson. One lesson may take 30-40 minutes depending on your familiarity with the Scriptures. You may want to do the lessons in shorter increments of time, depending on your schedule and personal preferences. I find that I absorb, retain, and apply the message of the Scriptures better when I am not rushed.

Please begin your study time with prayer. Ask the Holy Spirit to give you understanding of God's Word, as it is promised that He will do according to 1 Corinthians 2:12-13: "Now we have received, not the spirit of the world, but the Spirit who is from God, that we might know the things freely given to us by God, which things we also speak, not in words taught by human wisdom, but in those taught by the Spirit, combining spiritual thoughts with spiritual words." I have given you a reminder at the beginning of each lesson.

Observation, interpretation, and application. The Scripture readings, activities, cross-references and word definitions are all placed in the order which is most appropriate to your study. It is best to follow this order if you can, rather than skipping steps or setting steps aside to be completed at a different time. The order follows the inductive study process: observation (what the Scripture says), interpretation (what the author intended, what the Scripture means) and application (what difference the Scripture makes in your life). You will be doing the research, cross-referencing and summarization of the truths of each passage. When you finish a study of a passage, you will have gleaned more understanding on your own than you will find in some commentaries!

Looking up Hebrew word definitions. One of the activities included to help you understand the correct interpretation of the scripture is discovering and considering the definition of a word in its original language. Please make sure that you look up the definition of the word in its original language, not the definition of the English word. You will be given a prompt like this:

Meditate: Strong's #1897
Hebrew word:
Hebrew definition:

There are several ways you can look up the words given.

- You can google the Strong's reference number (Strong's 1897) and your web browser will give you links to the definition.
- You can go to an online Bible study website (recommendations below) and use their free reference materials. Look for "study" tabs, "lexicons" (this is what Hebrew and Greek word dictionaries are called), "concordances" and "original language" tools. There are search boxes where you can type in the Strong's reference number. Use H before the number for Hebrew words (H1897).
  studylight.org **blueletterbible.com** **biblestudytools.com**
  Suggested resources, described on page 178, are also available at these websites if you want to do more research on your own.
- You can download free Bible study apps such as **BibleHub** and **Blue Letter Bible** for your smartphone and/or tablet. I use **MySword** which allows me to go to a passage and click on the Strong's reference number next to the word. Try a few different ones and see what you like best.
- You may have some great resources on your own bookshelves! Enjoy using books like: *Strong's Exhaustive Concordance* and *The Complete Word Study Dictionary* by Spiros Zhodiates.

If you have trouble, it would be better to skip the exercise rather than filling in the English definition.

It's about your head and your heart. My hope is that you will read portions of Scripture and gain understanding of what is being communicated through them so that you can consider how to apply the truth of God's Word to your life. I have tried to make the study "user-friendly" and I promise that I don't ask trick questions. I do want to make you think hard sometimes though! I hope you won't get overwhelmed. Do what you can, a little bit at a time. The reward of knowing our holy God through His recorded word far outweighs the time and effort of study.

Prayer requests and praises. You will find pages at the end of this workbook which provide prompts from Scriptures for your prayers as well as a place for you to write out a personal prayer request . If you are studying with a group, it would be helpful to reflect on your personal prayer request before sharing it with the group. Keep your requests brief and personal. This page is also a place to record the prayer requests of others.

Lesson 1 ᔐ Job 1:1-50

WHO IS JOB ?

There are just no short, easy summaries for the book of Job. It is a book of difficult themes and topics and many of the words in this book are hard to define. But it is a powerful portion of our Scriptures, and I am so very thankful for it. There are grand truths and comforting perspectives contained in its verses. Everyone who suffers in some way can learn from the record of the suffering of Job. And the book of Job is not just about the man Job, but it is about the God of Job. I think that by the time our study of this book is complete, you will agree that the book of Job exalts the One and Only God as our wise and wonderful Creator and Protector and Comforter and Redeemer. We will say with Job: Blessed be the name of the Lord.

I don't expect too many easy study sessions from this book! I will do my best to keep our process of study as simple as possible because the material we will be studying will not be simple. Are you ready?

We are going to start by reading the introductory "backstory" given to us in the first two chapters of Job. We'll take plenty of time to understand the details in Job 1 and 2 over the next several lessons, but I think we should go ahead and begin to absorb the whole situation that the author lays out for us.

ᔐ Please pray for the Holy Spirit to give you understanding of God's Word. ᔐ

Please read Job 1:1-2:12.

Every time I read these chapters, I am stunned. Some aspect of this story catches my attention and makes me ponder it anew, no matter how many times I've read it before.

What about you? What has caught your attention and what are you pondering in this reading of Job 1:1-2:12?

I appreciate Warren Wiersbe's comments with which he begins his commentary on Job.

> Lord Byron was on target when he wrote, "Truth is always strange; stranger than fiction." The book of Job is not religious fiction. Job was a real person, not an imaginary character; both Ezekiel (14:14,20) and James (5:11) attest to that. Because he was a real man who had real experiences, he can tell us what we need to know about life and its problems in this real world.[1]

Let's learn about the real life of this real man, Job.

Where did he live, according to Job 1:1? _____________

Can you find that place on a world map today? Nope. Not even Google Maps can pinpoint it. But the prophet Jeremiah knew about it when he wrote that the Lord had sent him to the rulers of the nations, including all the kings of the land of Uz (Jeremiah.25:17-20).

What places did Jeremiah name in Lamentations 4:21?

Lamentations is poetry, and in Hebrew poetry one line is often parallel to the other line. This tells us that Edom and Uz were probably the same territory. My research has led me to understand that Uz was most likely in the area of Edom, or to its east or northeast; this would be somewhere in the area between today's southern Syria and in the Arabian peninsula. Because of Jeremiah's statements, what we can understand definitively is that Uz is not in the land of Egypt or Israel.

There are also many references throughout the book of Job that refer to places and customs of the Arabian peninsula, once again indicating that Uz was a real place and it was not in Israel or Egypt. And this means that Job was not an Israelite!

While we are considering the reality of Job and his homeland, please notice Noah's descendants named in Genesis 10:1, 21-23. Who were Noah's sons, grandsons, and great-grandsons? (Nations developed from these descendants.)

You might think there would have been something more interesting to begin with in our study than trying to locate or prove the reality of the land of Uz. But it's important right from the beginning to establish the truth of the record of Job. If Job were a fictional character, then other characters in his story might be considered fictional as well. There is nothing fictional about Satan or God.

Based on Job 1:1, what was the most important thing that the author wanted us to know about Job?

What does it mean when it says that Job was blameless and upright? Let's look at the meaning of these words in their original language.

Please look up the definition of the following words:
Blameless: Strong's #8535
Hebrew word:
Hebrew definition:

Upright: Strong's #3477
Hebrew word:
Hebrew definition:

Commentators suggest that the word "blameless" refers to Job's character and that the word "upright" refers to his actions. These two words used together to describe Job tell us that he was beyond reproach and they indicate the peak of moral perfection. He had integrity and his actions were carried out with integrity. Later in the book we will see Job's friends call him a wicked man and a hypocrite. He was nothing like that.

What is the hope and promise of a blameless and upright life, according to the verses below?
Psalm 25:20-22

Psalm 37:37

Job is also described as one who feared God and turned from evil.

Please look up the definitions for the following words:
Fear: Strong's #3373
Hebrew word:
Hebrew definition:

God: Strong's #430
Hebrew word:
Hebrew definition:

Turn: Strong's #5493
Hebrew word:
Hebrew definition:

I've already mentioned to you that Job was not an Israelite. That does impact our understanding of what it meant for Job to fear God. Nothing is mentioned in the book of Job about the Ten Commandments or any instructions that the Lord gave to the nation of Israel through Moses. However, Job knew enough about the One True God to know of His holiness and greatness and power and righteousness.

Job responded to the Lord with a holy awe, respect, and worship. He responded with actions that showed his reverence. He responded by having nothing to do with evil.

Does the statement that Job was "blameless and upright, one who feared God and turned from evil" mean that Job was sinless?

If our behavior matched the behavior of Job, would it mean that we are sinless?

How do the following verses answer that question?
Ecclesiastes 7:20

Romans 3:23

Romans 5:12

> These then are the four characteristics of Job's piety—he was sincere; upright; a worshipper of God; and one who abstained from all wrong. These are the essential elements of true religion everywhere; and the whole statement in the book of Job shows Job was, though not absolutely free from the sins which cleave to our nature, eminent in each of these things.[2]

As we have briefly touched on the sin nature that each of us are born with, let us also take note of the rescue from that sin that God has provided in Jesus Christ.

What does 2 Corinthians 5:21 tell us?

What does 1 John 3:5 say?

As ethical and moral and reverential as Job was, he was still just a man with a sin problem. And he knew it. We will see that he knew that he needed help from someone to bring him into a right relationship with his holy God. We cannot imitate Job's integrity and think that we'll be just fine. Each of us has the need to be rescued from our sin and brought into a personal relationship with God.

If you have recognized your sin problem, and turned away from it, and trusted that Jesus became sin and died on the cross to take away your sin, then you have been forgiven and cleansed!

We've now met the man Job and learned the most critical information about him. In our next lesson we'll learn a little more about his family and social standing. Life is going really well for Job right now.

Lesson 2 ∾ Job 1:2-5

THE GREATEST OF ALL THE PEOPLE

I hope that this section of our study will help you come to care for Job in a tender way. I already respect him and am inspired by his fear of the Lord. The next description of his life will add another dimension to our understanding of the kind of man he was. We'll find out what the narrator of the story emphasizes, and we'll also find out what Job says about himself.

∾ Please pray for understanding of the Scriptures inspired by the Holy Spirit. ∾

Please read Job 1:1-5.

His family consisted of: ___________ sons and ______________ daughters.

This big family was a blessing! In Hebrew thought, seven and three are numbers that indicate completeness.

His estate consisted of:

_______________ sheep (providing luxurious clothing and ample food)
_______________ camels (giving him transportation)
_______________ pairs of oxen (used by servants to plow the ground and provide food)
_______________ female donkeys (good for milk, breeding, and riding)
And _________________

All this made him (according to Job 1:3): ____

Do the math . . . how many total animals did Job possess? ________________

I'm not crazy about all those animals, but I do think it's quite fascinating information. This report on Job's property tells us about his wealth, as well as where he lived and when he lived.

Because he owned sheep and oxen, he most likely lived in a permanent location, in the city of that day, rather than being a nomad roaming the desert. Job's wealth was measured in livestock as it was in the days of Abraham and Jacob, so we assume that he lived during their time in history. He may have even known one of them!

We will place Job on the timeline of history at about 1900 BC, which was after the flood, after the event at the Tower of Babel, and during the lifetime of Jacob and Esau and their children..

Now let's consider those days of feasting, which might have been birthday celebrations. What does Job 1:4-5 tell you about his family's home life and his heart?

Job acted as a priest for his children. He interceded on their behalf. He prayed for them. The passage does not tell us how they might have cursed God. It just tells us that this was Job's greatest concern and he took action before God for the sake of his sons and daughters. Job's care for his family is highlighted here as a very good thing.

How often do you intercede on behalf of your family members—whether they are in your home or have their own? Are your prayers related to defending God's reputation in their lives? Take time to pray for them now.

While we are meeting Job and finding out how he lived, I would like you to see how he described his actions himself. We're going to look ahead at what he had to say in the midst of his longest speech after he listened to all the perspectives of his friends.

What does Job 28:28 say that God has said to man?

That should sound familiar. The very characteristics with which Job was described in Job 1:1 are repeated as God's instructions for wisdom.

Job was a wise man and behaved as one. In Job 29, in the midst of his suffering, he recalls what life was like before incredible disaster came upon him.

Please read Job 29:1-25 and note below how Job described the following aspects of his life:[3]
Enjoying the presence of God (v.2-6)

Receiving respect from others (v.7-11)

Ministry to others (v.12-17)

Confidence in his future (v.18-20)

Speaking words of encouragement and help (v.21-25)

This is an autobiography of Job's life. It was so good! It was so blessed! He thought it would always be that way.

Let's begin to do something that we will continue to do throughout our study. I will give you reminders to recognize the Lord's blessings and to praise Him in all circumstances.

I hope this exercise will train us to honor the Lord, thank Him, and trust Him, no matter what we are experiencing.

Thank You Lord for Your blessing of ____

____

~Blessed be the Name of the Lord.~

Lesson 3 ~ Job 1:6-12

WHO IS SATAN?

"Now there was a day when the sons of God came to present themselves before the Lord." Job 1:6 Without any transition, the narrator of Job's story tells us about a particular day in Heaven. It is fascinating! What is described is the regular activity around the throne of God. The sons of God are angels, and they are appearing before the Lord to report their activities and receive instruction.

~ Please pray for the Holy Spirit to give you understanding of God's Word. ~

Note how the following passages describe angels' activities and attitudes in Heaven:
1 Kings 22:19-22

Psalm 89:5-7

Psalm 103:20-22

Daniel 7:9-10

Revelation 5:11-13

Now that we've looked at the appropriate behavior of heavenly beings before the Lord, let's consider the attitude and activity of Satan described in the book of Job.

Please read Job 1:6-12.

What does this passage tell you about Satan's access to heaven and his access to the earth?

J. Vernon McGee says this:

By the way, Satan must also make a report. That is amazing, isn't it? Do you think he came from hell? No, he didn't. Friends, hell hasn't been opened up yet. No one is in hell today. It will not be opened up until the Millennium takes place on this earth. Hell is the place prepared for the Devil and his angels, but they are not there yet. The fact of the matter is that Satan has as much access to the earth as you and I have, and more so.[4]

But Satan is not free to do whatever he wants to whomever he wants.

What details in Job 1:6-12 indicate that Satan is under God's authority and must submit to Him?

In the midst of this encounter, the Lord brings attention to "His servant Job." He repeats the narrator's description that Job is a blameless and upright man who fears God and turns from evil. And the Lord adds His divine approval of him saying, "there is none like him on the earth." Satan does not respond with praise for God or his servant. Instead, he challenges Job's motives in worshipping God—as if he only does so because of God's blessings. But ultimately Satan is challenging the very nature of God—as if He is not worthy of being worshiped for Who He is.

The attack is on God through Job, and the only way the Accuser can be proven false is through Job.[5]

Please look up the definition for the following word:
Satan: Strong's #7854
Hebrew word:
Hebrew definition:

What do the following verses tell us about Satan's access to God, his attitude and his activities?
Zechariah 3:1-2

Luke 22:31

1 Peter 5:8-9

Revelation 12:10

What are the other names or descriptions of Satan, according to the following verses?
Isaiah 14:12

Matthew 12:24

Matthew 13:39

John 8:44

John 12:31

Ephesians 2:2

2 Corinthians 4:4

Now that we have an understanding of the evil enemy of the Lord, let's look again at his interaction with our sovereign God. While you notice the facts, please also notice Satan's lack of reverence for the Lord.

What are the facts about Job that Satan is aware of, according to Job 1:9-10?

What does Satan demand and expect, according to Job 1:11?

What is the first word uttered by the Lord in Job 1:12? ___________________

This word should have an exclamation point after it! It is an interjection demanding attention! Look! See! It emphasizes the phrase that follows it. The Lord responds to Satan's challenge and says, "Now hear this! All that is Job's . . . everything that he has and everything that he owns…all that I have given him, all is in your power. You can do what you want, just don't touch Job himself."

This is shocking. This is hard to accept. The God who declares His unfailing love repeatedly throughout the Scriptures also declares that His faithful servant Job can be attacked by the most powerful, evil creature in the universe. Just don't forget: Satan is on a leash.

Please re-read Job 1:1-12 and respond to the following questions:

Does a faithful, God-fearing life guarantee a life without suffering? Why or why not?

What is Satan's goal?

Can we understand why God allows suffering to fulfill His purposes?

These are very sobering questions to ponder. One of the most often asked and debated questions in life has been: why do bad things happen to good people? Here in the book of Job, we find two answers to that question. Satan wants it. God allows it.

The book of Job is going to show us that when God allows suffering in the lives of one of His servants, He has a purpose. As we study this book, we'll see how we are to respond during the suffering and what we can hope for when it's all over.

These topics are so deep and incomprehensible. They actually bring me to a point of thinking—why ask why? Just let God be God, and go with whatever He lets happen, and trust Him.

Thank You Lord for Your blessing of ____

____

∾Blessed be the Name of the Lord.∾

Lesson 4 ∾ Job 1:13-22

THE END OF LIFE AS HE KNEW IT

If you are a little bit worried about studying the events that are about to unfold in Job's life, I understand. We've already learned that God will allow Satan to touch all that Job has. And now we are going to discover how he does that. We're going to study disasters that will break our hearts.

ఌ Please pray for understanding of the Scriptures inspired by the Holy Spirit. ఌ

Please read Job 1:1-22. (We keep going back to the beginning so we can be reminded of the things we've already learned.)

On what day did disaster strike Job's family and estate?

Is there any day that is safe from harm? We have to say no. It is especially hard when pain and suffering come on days that we expect to be special, happy celebrations. My friend's father died on Christmas Day.

What truth in Psalm 31:15-16 is our hope and our prayer for the days of our lives?

Sometimes the response to disaster is to give the details of it, and just admit that it has happened. Four messengers rushed to bring the bad news to Job.

Please record in the chart below, the details of the tragedies in Job's life, according to Job 1:14-19. (Note the numbers based on Job 1:2-3)

Messenger	Cause of Disaster	Type of Loss	Number of Dead or Stolen	Survivors
1				
2				
3				
4				

A messenger came to Job . . . while he was still speaking, another came also...while he was still speaking, another came also . . . while he was still speaking, another came also. There have been countless terrible tragedies throughout the history of the earth, but I can't imagine that there has ever been anyone who has experienced the magnitude of the losses that Job suffered that day.

The Lord had said to Satan, "Behold! All that he has is in your power; only do not lay a hand on his person." We know that Satan was the force behind the thieves and murderers and lightening storm and the tornado. But Job didn't know it. And knowing it would not have made the grief any less.

Oh. This is so horrible.

As I am writing this lesson, I have been made aware of a car crash that took the life of a sweet 18-year-old only daughter. Her parents, our community, and her friends are grieving over her loss. Her senior year in high school had just begun. Her senior portraits are beautiful. One person described this tragic accident as something that changed the color of the world.

Think of a time when you suffered some type of loss. How did you feel physically, emotionally, and spiritually?

What did Job do in response to this catastrophe, according to Job 1:20?

-

In the ripping of his robe he is announcing his horrible grief…. [And] he "shaved his head." The hair is always pictured in the Scriptures as the glory of an individual, an expression of his worth. The shaving of the head, therefore, is symbolic of the loss of personal glory. [6]

Grief is not fun. Of all the emotions that we can feel, I think we would choose anything besides grief. Anger, fear, embarrassment, jealousy . . . those are not fun but they are easier to feel and express than grief. The pain of loss is shocking, numbing, debilitating, and can be paralyzing. Grief does need an outlet though, and it is appropriate and healthy to express it. That's what Job did. And in the midst of his expressions of grief, he worshipped God.

Please look up the definition of the following word:
Worshipped: Strong's #7812
Hebrew word:
Hebrew definition:

The same word above is used in the verses below. Please note the reason for the worship.
Joshua 5:14

Psalm 5:7

Psalm 99:5

Please write out Job's words of worship found in Job 1:21.

Have you had a time where you've worshipped the Lord with these words? Can you worship Him with them today?

Satan wanted Job to curse God to His face. Instead, Job reverentially bowed before his God and blessed Him.

Please look up the definition for the following words:
Bless: Strong's #1288
Hebrew word:
Hebrew definition:

Name: Strong's #8034
Hebrew word:
Hebrew definition:

LORD: Strong's #3068
Hebrew word:
Hebrew definition:

I think these three words are the heartbeat of Job. He adored and praised God. He knew the honor and reputation of God. And he understood that his God was the eternal, self-existent, mysterious, and personal God. Later, we will see Job defend the reputation of God before his friends; and as he does so, he will be blessing, not cursing, God's name before his audience of Satan as well.

What is the final comment about Job at this point in the story? How does Job 1:22 relate to Job 1:1, 5 and 8?

What is the promise for people like Job, according to James 1:12?

Chuck Swindoll encourages his readers to try to imitate Job's position. He says, "Palms down, facedown, knees and toes touching the ground, body fully extended, as you pour out your heart in worship. It's the position Job deliberately took. Complete and humble submission."[7] I encourage you to end today's lesson with this posture of worship and whatever words of blessing the Lord your heart desires.

Thank You Lord for Your blessing of ____

____

Blessed be the Name of the Lord.

Lesson 5 ∾ Job 2:1-9

SATAN STRIKES AGAIN

The more time we spend with Job, the more we will grasp how terrible his suffering was. Now that we've studied the first tragedy brought on by Satan's challenge to God, it is sobering to read about the prosperity of his life before the disaster. We will consider the second attack on Job in this lesson, but we need to start at the beginning of the story again. The information that we are given in Job 1 and 2 is critical to our understanding of the rest of the book.

∾ Please pray for the Holy Spirit to give you understanding of God's Word. ∾

Please read Job 1:1-5.
How would you describe Job's life and behavior in your own words?

Please read Job 1:6-12.
How would you explain the dialogue between the Lord and Satan in your own words?

Please read Job 1:13-22.
How would you summarize the calamity Job experienced and his response to it?

Please read Job 2:1-9 below. Using 4 colors, highlight the phrases that are identical to Job 1:6-12. Underline the phrases that are different. Circle the words: integrity and curse.

Job 2:1-9[NKJ] Again there was a day when the sons of God came to present themselves before the LORD, and Satan came also among them to present himself before the LORD. [2]And the LORD said to Satan, "From where do you come?" So Satan answered the LORD and said, "From going to and fro on the earth, and from walking back and forth on it." [3]Then the LORD said to Satan, "Have you considered My servant Job, that there is none like him on the earth, a blameless and upright man, one who fears God and shuns evil? And still he holds fast to his integrity, although you incited Me against him, to destroy him without cause." [4]So Satan answered the LORD and said, "Skin for skin! Yes, all that a man has he will give for his life. [5]But stretch out Your hand now, and touch his bone and his flesh, and he will surely curse You to Your face!" [6]And the LORD said to Satan, "Behold, he is in your hand, but spare his life." [7]So Satan went out from the presence of the LORD, and struck Job with painful boils from the sole of his foot to the crown of his head. [8]And he took for himself a potsherd with which to scrape himself while he sat in the midst of the ashes. [9]Then his wife said to him, "Do you still hold fast to your integrity? Curse God and die!" [10]But he said to her, "You speak as one of the foolish women speaks. Shall we indeed accept good from God, and shall we not accept adversity?" In all this Job did not sin with his lips.

Have you wondered why the Lord asks Satan, "where have you come from?" Let's remember that God is omniscient (all-knowing), omnipresent (present everywhere), and omnipotent (all-powerful). And God never changes; He is the same yesterday, today, and tomorrow. He asks Satan questions to force him to speak. God is in control.

Answer the questions below based on Job 2:1-6.
Did Satan give a full and honest answer to the Lord's question "where have you come from?" What should he have said?

In both dialogues between the Lord and Satan (Job 1:6-12 and Job 2:1-6), Satan only speaks when asked a question. I've got to tell you, that's a fact that makes me smile. Satan does not have the freedom to spout off his mouth in the face of our holy, wonderful God! However, when Satan does speak, it is with hostile, short, vague, disrespectful language. That's not surprising.

What does the Lord's question and declaration about Job tell you about the Lord, about Job, and about Satan?

Who does the Lord indicate is to blame for Job's suffering?

The two answers to the two questions above must give us a perspective to consider when someone we know or even we ourselves ask why God has let a trial happen to us. Sometimes there is not a particular sin in our lives causing pain and suffering. Sometimes there is. But sometimes God allows difficulties when there is no reason for it in us.

How do the following verses support the idea that God allows trials for reasons other than sin in a person's life?
John 9:2-3

John 11:32-45

1 Peter 1:6-7

What is your response to this truth, regarding the wisdom and sovereignty of God, that He can and will do or allow whatever He thinks is best in our lives, whether we like it or not?

What is Satan's perverted perspective of Job in Job 2:4?

Job's praise of the Lord's name and the Lord's praise of Job's integrity infuriated Satan. He harshly accused Job of accepting the deaths of all of his children, servants, and livestock as long as he could keep his own life. Even in the very presence of our omniscient God, Satan twists the truth. I'm so thankful that the Lord doesn't listen to a thing Satan says about me.

What does Satan want and what does the Lord allow, according to Job 2:5-6? (Note the difference.)

> If Job is deprived of existence altogether the question will remain forever unsettled; for everything hangs upon Job's reaction. So the man himself must be smitten and smitten so severely that he despairs of life and feels himself in the grip of death, but he must not actually die.[8]

What is the second tragedy that Job experiences, according to the following verses?

Job 2:7-8	Job 19:17
Job 2:12	Job 19:20
Job 3:24	Job 30:17
Job 7:4	Job 30:27
Job 7:5	Job 30:30
Job 9:18	Job 33:21
Job 16:16	

Some people endure illness better than others. I'm a wimp. If I'm miserable, or even if I just have a little ache here or there, I'll let you know about it. I am overwhelmed at the physical pain that Job suffered. In case you're wondering, no one really knows exactly what the correct diagnosis was of his disease. Possibilities include: smallpox, elephantiasis, chronic eczema, keratosis, or even melanoma—aggressive skin cancer.[9] *Apparently, and sadly, the only so-called relief that Job could get was from scratching himself with a broken piece of pottery while he sat in a slump at the city garbage dump.*

According to Job 2:9, what did Job's wife say that corresponded to the Lord's statement about Job and Satan's goal for Job?

Not knowing the limitation God had put on the Accuser, Job's wife at this point diagnosed the disease as incurable and recommended that he curse God and die (v.9). Chrysostom's explanation of why Satan did not destroy Job's wife with the rest of the family was so that she could become his tool. Job's mental anguish was certainly intensified by his wife's advice. Had he followed it, the contest would have ended with the Accuser as the victor. [10]

How did Job continue to maintain his integrity, according to Job 2:10?

We'll study Job's response more closely in our next lesson. For now, we will end with some reflections on Job's wife.

Based on all that we have studied so far, what had Job's wife experienced?

Please notice how wise and kind Job was regarding his wife. (Fill in the blank in the following sentence with one word.)

He said that she spoke ________ foolish women speak, not that she **was** a foolish woman.

We need to realize that trials bring out the best and the worst in each of us. That's kind of the point, sometimes! Mrs. Job wasn't the one that the Lord pointed out to Satan. Job's trial would also do some refining work on her. For anyone going through a trial, but especially for our closest family and friends, we need to stand firm in faithfulness to the Lord with them, not against them.

What are some things you could say to someone in the midst of a difficult or painful situation to inspire their confidence and encourage them?

Blessed be the Name of the Lord.

Lesson 6 ᔓ Job 2:10-13

MAINTAINING INTEGRITY

What earns a purple heart, a medal of honor, or the distinction of being called a hero? What attitude is so humble and so sincere that it causes great respect and applause? What did God highlight in the life of Job that was worthy of heavenly honor? What did Satan and Job's wife, and eventually Job's friends try to make Job lose? You know the answer. In one word: Integrity.

I'd like to consider the concept of integrity before we enter the rest of the story.

ᔓ Please pray for understanding of the Scriptures inspired by the Holy Spirit. ᔓ

Once again, please read the prologue of the book of Job. Read Job 1:1-2:13.

What did the Lord say regarding Job's integrity, in Job 2:3?

The Hebrew word for integrity is based on the same root word as blameless. They mean the same thing. You noted in our first lesson that blameless means completely moral and ethically pure. Job was wholehearted in his commitment to God and His ways. What he said and what he did and what he thought were in sync. His behavior was above reproach and there was no hypocrisy in him.

And then, in the face of incomprehensible catastrophe, he held fast to his integrity.

Please look up the definition for the following word:
Hold fast: Strong's #2388
Hebrew word:
Hebrew definition:

Based on the definition above, do you think Job just happened to hold fast to his integrity or did he make a decision to do so?

Please write out the two statements that Job made that gave evidence of Job's integrity. See Job 1:21 and Job 2:10.

These two statements reflect both sides of the same coin. What are the basic truths that you can observe from them? (Try to make at least 4 statements.)

Please look up the definition of the following word:
Adversity: Strong's #7451
Hebrew word:
Hebrew definition:

Does it surprise you that this is the same word used when describing that Job turned away from evil? That which Job made intentional choices to avoid, that evil behavior or attitude that he shunned, the mischief, trouble, and wickedness that he stayed far away from was all turned back on him by the maliciousness of Satan. And God allowed it.

Let's look at some important aspects of God's character. Note what you learn from the following verses:
Exodus 15:11

Isaiah 55:9

Jeremiah 10:6-7

Romans 11:33-34

Please use the truths of the verses above as the basis for a prayer, blessing the name of the Lord, whether you are in the midst of a trial or you realize that God may allow one to come into your life.

Blessed be the Name of the Lord.

Absolutely sovereign yet infinitely wise, God's ways are perfect. Thus, we can trust Him. When tragedy strikes, there are no explanations sent from God explaining *why* such an ordeal has just been unleashed upon our lives. In the midst of life's tragedies, when we most want answers, so often there are none. In these difficult hours we must simply trust God. [11]

We must simply trust God. And hold fast to our integrity. There is a passage of Scripture that I hope will be encouraging to you as a summary of standing firm as Job did in the midst of an onslaught of spiritual wickedness.

Please read Ephesians 6:10-18.
How are we to be strong?

What are we to be aware of?

What aspects of the armor of God did Job take up? (Focus on the attributes of the armor, rather than the soldier's clothing.)

We have begun our climb to the high places in our first lessons on the book of Job. Chapters 1 and 2 contain profound, mysterious, bewildering concepts. I expect that you have begun to wrestle with difficult issues, just as I have. I come to this study with a lifetime of growing in my faith in the Lord, and I am still learning to trust Him no matter what He gives to me or takes from me. I have seen His faithfulness through the good and the bad. I have been bombarded with spiritual warfare and have lost a few battles. But I have also had victory in Jesus!

I have been most encouraged when I focus on the holiness and sovereignty of my God and the grace of my Savior. I want to bless the name of the Lord and exasperate His adversary!

> When the bad as well as the good is received at the hand of God, every experience of life becomes an occasion of blessing. But the cost is high. It is easier to lower your view of God than to raise your faith to such a height.[12]

Will you join me in the adventure of exercising and stretching and raising our faith to greater heights than we've known before? Please describe the type of faith that you would like to have.

Good for you. God is for you. He is going to do great things in our lives!

Now, we've got just a little bit more in the prologue of Job to consider. It's kind of good news, in the midst of the bad. The bad news about Job's tragic circumstances traveled far and wide prompting a visit from some friends.

According to Job 2:11:
Who came to see Job? Where were they from?

Why did they come?

According to Job 2:12:
How did Job's suffering affect his friends?

According to Job 2:13:
How did the friends comfort Job upon their arrival?

To their credit, Job's friends traveled long distances, gave up a great deal of their time, and approached Job with good intentions. They sat with him in his misery and mourned with him over the deaths of his children as well as over the loss of everything else he had. Their silence was their show of sympathy. You may already know it was their best moment, because when they open their mouths later in the story, they say all the wrong things.

Some people are better than others at empathizing with the grief of another. Someone told me once that I have "sympathy tears." It is hard to comprehend or enter into the deep pain of another when you have not been through the same situations. But no one's experiences are identical to another's . . . so we all need to be careful and sensitive on every occasion.

How do the following verses instruct us regarding our perspectives and actions during times of the suffering of others?
Ecclesiastes 3:4

Matthew 7:12

Romans 12:15

Colossians 3:12

Please close today's lesson with a final prayer of blessing the Lord through the verse below.

2 Corinthians 1:3-4 Blessed be the God and Father of our Lord Jesus Christ, the Father of mercies and God of all comfort, who comforts us in all our affliction, so that we may be able to comfort those who are in any affliction, with the comfort with which we ourselves are comforted by God.

Lesson 7 ~ Overview and Job 3

THE BIG VIEW AND THE BLACK VIEW

I think it's fairly common to search for something normal and routine to help give a bit of relief from the intensity of grief. Perhaps cleaning the bathroom or walking the dog or watching a movie is something you have done to cope with the pain of suffering. I received some shocking news recently and while I was waiting for more information, I swam laps. I needed to do something, and the water was a perfect place to pray.

While we haven't actually been experiencing the tragic events of Job's life, we have been thinking about them and thinking about hard-to-grasp truths of God's sovereignty as well. I think it's time to do something a little routine. Because Job's suffering and deep topics are going to be our constant focus, we'll probably need times like this every now and then!

So—let's get a bit of exercise. Let's take a little walk through the book of Job, so that you can get familiar with its structure. I want you to have an idea of what's coming.

ᔓ Please pray for the Holy Spirit to give you understanding of God's Word. ᔓ

Please fill in the chart below.

	Location (heaven or earth)	**Participants in Dialogue**
Job 1:1-5		
Job 1:6-12		
Job 1:13-22		
Job 2:1-6		
Job 2:7-13		

Job 1 and 2 are called the prologue. They are written in prose while the rest of the book is poetry until the epilogue. The description of Job and the scenes in heaven are given to us by the "narrator." The author of the book of Job is unnamed, but it is possible that Job himself wrote the book.

What does Job say in Job 19:23?

That's why my vote is for Job as the author!

Whoever composed the book of Job was a genius, inspired by the Spirit of God. This book consists of 42 chapters, 40 of which are poetry and contain the dialogues between Job and his three friends, plus the exhortation of a young man and then the powerful words of the Lord.

Please turn to the first verse of each section in the outline below and record the speaker.

Prologue Job 1:1-2:12
Dialogues
Opening Lament
Job 3:1-26 ____________________________

First Series of Speeches
Job 4:1-5:27___________________________
Job 6:1-7:21___________________________
Job 8:1-22_____________________________
Job 9:1-10:22 __________________________
Job 11:1-20____________________________
Job 12:1-14:22 _________________________

Second Series of Speeches
Job 15:1-35____________________________
Job 16:1-17:16 _________________________
Job 18:1-21 ____________________________
Job 19:1-29 ____________________________
Job 20:1-29____________________________
Job 21:1-34 ____________________________

Third Series of Speeches
Job 22:1-30 ____________________________
Job 23:1-24:25__________________________
Job 25:1-6 _____________________________

Monologue
Job 26:1-31:40__________________________

Monologue
Job 32:1-37:24 _________________________

Monologue
Job 38:1-40:2 __________________________

Response
Job 40:3-5_____________________

Job 40:6-41:34__________________________

Response
Job 42:1-6 _____________________

Epilogue Job 42:7-17

Highlight the different speakers in the outline above using a different color for each speaker. (You'll need 6 colors!)

As I prepared for this study, I printed the whole book of Job on plain white paper, with each speaker in a different colored font. It has been so helpful! I always know when Job is speaking because his words are blue. It may be hard for me to read the book of Job in my Bible from now on if I don't color-code the speeches!

We've seen the big view of the book of Job. Now we'll see the black view of Job himself.

How many times have you wondered: what was Moses, or Mary, or Peter thinking? How did they feel in their situation? Job leaves no room for doubt. He opens up and tells us his deepest thoughts and emotions. Keep in mind as you read them that his words have been captured in poetry.

Please read Job 3:1-26.

What critically important point is made in Job 3:1, showing that Job still maintains his integrity?

What's his basic perspective in this speech?

The poetic nature of this lament makes a few of his comments hard to understand. Why does he mention Leviathan—a violent sea monster? He seems to think that if an enchanter had the power to summon the monster from the depths of the sea, he could also have the power to curse a day.[13] *When referring to his wish that he had been stillborn or miscarried, he asks why he wasn't "hidden" —meaning buried. And without mentioning it by name, he refers to Sheol—the grave, as "there," which is where he wishes he were.*

There are four desperate desires that Job expresses. Note them according to the verses below:
Job 3:3-5

Job 3:6-10

Job 3:11-15

Job 3:20-23

Notice that none of his statements even hint at the consideration of taking his own life. He is at the extreme end of black despair and does not want to be alive; but in his continued integrity and fear of God, he does not speak of suicide. He wants God to take his life but he will not take his life into his own hands.

What emotions and concerns does Job give voice to in Job 3:20-26? What is he feeling?

He is absolutely exhausted from grief and illness. He is utterly miserable and desperate for relief. He is despondent and spiritually depressed. He did what you surely have done in difficult times. He asked "why?" And no one but God had the answers.

It's easy to ask why but difficult to get the right answer. There is nothing wrong with asking why, as long as we don't get the idea that God *owes* us an answer.[14]

A key phrase in verse 23 is "whom God has hedged in." This is the same word used in Satan's challenge to God and means the same thing in both places. God put a hedge, a fence, a boundary around Job for his protection before the tragic events of his life, during the first attack of Satan, and even during the second evil assault on his body. God protected Job from death.

We know why God spared his life. It was so that the faithful servant Job could prove that the Lord is worthy of praise no matter what.

Do you believe that God has put a hedge of protection around you? How does this affect your understanding of the circumstances of your life?

Please write out Job's last two statements from Job 3:25-26.

Job expressed his agony out loud. He was honest with himself and his friends and his God. Job 3 has been called one of the most depressing chapters of the Bible. But it is invaluable in teaching us that if a person with the integrity and faith of Job can fall into dark depression, then so can we.

Do you know the importance of sharing your deepest, darkest pain and grief with someone who will give you comfort and truth according to God's word? Are you willing to be a safe place for someone to spill his or her guts out?

The last word of Job's lament is "trouble" or "turmoil," depending on your translation. He says it comes and keeps coming and coming and coming.

Turmoil (rogez) is a Hebrew noun derived from a verb meaning to shake or quake. Here it is used to express agitation or restlessness. It was also used of a person who was deeply disturbed emotionally.[15]

Not only did Job have the sadness of losing his dearly beloved children and not only did he have the life-changing loss of his business and wealth, but he also had the burden of wrestling with his perspective on how he could have or should have lived his life differently.

These are the kind of questions that wreak havoc on our peace: What have I done wrong? How could I have prevented this from happening? What would I do differently if I could live that day over again? How will I go on? How can I live like this? What do I do now? Why did God let this happen? Why did God let me live? Why did God let them die?

These questions are left unanswered in Job's life. And many times in our own.

Thank You Lord for Your blessing of ____

____

ᔓBlessed be the Name of the Lord.ᔓ

Lesson 8 ᔓ Job 4

AND NOW A WORD FROM HIS FRIEND

Woody, the little cowboy in Disney's movie Toy Story, was a great friend to his fellow playmates and to the little boy that loved him. Here's his perspective:

You've got a friend in me
You've got a friend in me

When the road looks rough ahead
And you're miles and miles from your nice warm bed
You just remember what your old pal said

Girl, you've got a friend in me
Yeah, you've got a friend in me
You've got a friend in me
You've got a friend in me

You've got troubles and I've got 'em too
There isn't anything I wouldn't do for you
We stick together and see it through
'Cause you've got a friend in me
You've got a friend in me [16]

It seems to me that Woody was the kind of friend that Job needed. But Eliphaz the Temanite was of a different disposition. He's going to make three long speeches to Job, speaking up and speaking his mind more than Bildad and Zophar. He's quite confident in his assessment of Job's character and the ways of God. Some of what he says sounds pretty good. But—beware. His premise is all wrong; so his application of truth is all wrong too. Let's sort out what Eliphaz has to say to Job. And don't forget what he has just heard spill out of Job's grieving heart.

∾ Please pray for the Holy Spirit to give you understanding of God's Word. ∾

Please read Job 3:1-26 and Job 4:1-5:27.

What do Job 4:1-2 and Job 5:27 tell you about the attitude and perspective of Eliphaz?

As I read Eliphaz's lecture, I kept thinking: poor Job! He wasn't hearing soothing words. There was no acknowledgement of his pain, no sympathy, no comfort. There was only accusation! Everything that Eliphaz said was an attack on the integrity of Job, whether he said it directly or indirectly. Keep in mind that Job had said nothing in his lamentation about his own innocence or guilt.

Briefly summarize Eliphaz's assertions according to the verses below:
Job 4:3-5

Job 4:6-9

Job 4:17

Job 5:1

Job 5:6-7

Job 5:8-16

Job 5:17

> But what Satan could not do with all his Sabeans, and all his Chaldeans, and all his winds from the wilderness to help him, that he soon did with the debating approaches and the controversial assaults of Eliphaz, and Zophar, and Bildad, and Elihu. Oh, the unmitigable curse of controversy![17]

Never before in my reading of the speech of Eliphaz did I notice the hiss of Satan. But after our intensive study of the first chapters of Job and being keenly aware of Job's upright character and Satan's evil goal, I see that Satan is using every possible circumstance to cause Job to curse God. Satan attacked Job's wealth, his family, his health, and his wife. And now he attacks his integrity through the limited perspective of Job's friends.

The words of Eliphaz carry the same skepticism and skewed truth as the words of Satan spoken to the Lord in Job 1-2 and spoken to Eve in Genesis 3. "Did God really say . . . ?" "You will be like God."

What is wrong with the statement made in Job 4:6? What do we need to remember from the following verses?
Job 2:3

Proverbs 3:25-26

Proverbs 14:26

1 Timothy 4:10

1 Peter 1:3-6

What is wrong with the statement in Job 4:7? Note the truths in the verses below:
Regarding death: Ecclesiastes 7:15 and 9:2

Regarding disaster: Luke 13:3-5

Regarding the death of an innocent man: Luke 23:46-47 and Hebrews 7:26-27

What is wrong with the "visions of the night" in Job 4:13-21? Just as Satan quoted a bit of truth when tempting Christ, Eliphaz also said a few things that were absolutely accurate: Job 4:17 is true according to Romans 3:32: all have sinned and fall short of the glory of God. Job 4:18 is true according to 2 Peter 2:4: angels rebelled against God. Job 4:19 is true according to Genesis 2:7: man was made out of dust. And Job 4:19-20 is true according to Psalm 90:10: life is short and hard.

But several aspects of Eliphaz's account should cause us to at least be hesitant in trusting its message. There was no mention that it was "the word of the Lord," which was the basis of the divine authority of a declaration. There was no comfort to "fear not," which was a common statement from God's awesome angels. There was a distorted question: "can a man be more righteous than God?" Some commentators say this question should be translated as: "can a mortal be righteous in God's perspective?" Either way, Job was not seeking equality with or exaltation over God, so this was not the issue. There was also a blatant lie: "they perish forever with no one regarding."

The truth is: The Lord looks down from heaven; He sees all the children of man; from where He sits enthroned, He looks out on all the inhabitants of the earth, He who fashions the hearts of them all and observes all their deeds. Psalm 33:13-15[HCSB]

How can you discern the truth or error in perspectives of authors, speakers, preachers, professors, philosophers, scientists and friends?

Does a "spiritual experience" guarantee that a message is from the Lord, according to 2 Corinthians 11:13-15?

Let's look at what Eliphaz said that might have been his way of cheering up Job. In Job 5:8 he says, as for me, I would seek God. And then in Job 5:17 he says, happy is the man whom God corrects. So, Eliphaz is saying—hey Job, you need to turn to God, accept His discipline, repent, turn from your sin, and you'll have a wonderful, happy life.

But Eliphaz doesn't have a clue on what's really happening to Job. We do. Eliphaz is so right and so wrong at the same time! Everything that he says in Job 5:9-18 is true about God. It's just not true about Job!

What is most meaningful to you right now about God's character as described in Job 5:9-18?

I mentioned earlier that Eliphaz said nothing comforting, kind or sympathetic. Let's end our lesson considering how to respond to someone in pain. The first lesson we can learn from Eliphaz is to realize that we may not know the reason for someone's suffering. Even knowing the truth about God may not give us the accurate evaluation of the truth of a situation.

What's good and what's bad according to Proverbs 15:4?

What is emphasized about Jesus in Matthew 14:14?

What is most important, according to 1 Corinthians 13:1?

How does Paul counsel believers in Colossians 3:8-14? Consider how appropriate his instruction is, especially when listening to and trying to encourage someone who is suffering.

Please read Job's words of grief once more, in Job 3. And let's practice responding to him according to the counsel of the verses above. What would you say to Job?

Perhaps your mother taught you a little etiquette about being eloquent: if you can't say something nice, don't say anything at all. Chuck Swindoll adds some godly wisdom to that advice, "if you don't have God's clear mind and indisputable facts to prove it, please just love your hurting friend and keep quiet."[18]

When friends' words are hard to hear, or you don't know what to say to your hurting friend, it's still right and helpful to turn to the Lord.

Thank You Lord for Your blessing of ______________________________________

____

ᔓBlessed be the Name of the Lord.ᔓ

Lesson 9 ᔓ Job 6 and 7

DISCOURAGEMENT, DEFENSIVENESS, AND MORE DEATH WISHES

Are you ready to hear Job's response to his friend? He's going to say exactly what he's thinking and feeling. In our last lesson, we learned that a hurting person needs a hug and not harassment. That's pretty much what Job will say.

In this outpouring of Job's soul, we'll be reminded of how utterly miserable he is. The only thing he's hoping for, the only thing he thinks will relieve his suffering, is death. He absolutely loathes his life. In addition to his material losses, family losses, and health losses, he thinks he has lost all purpose in life. The reverse is actually what is true. His life is eternally significant. He just doesn't know it.

By the way, there's a sea monster mentioned in Job 7:12! Job wonders if God thinks Job is as dangerous as one of those.

ᔓ Please pray for understanding of the Scriptures inspired by the Holy Spirit. ᔓ

Please read Job 6 and 7.

How would you describe Job's attitude expressed in this speech?

What observations can we make about the impact of grief on a person's words, based on Job 6:2-3, and Job 7:11?

A few commentators mention that Job is actually acknowledging that he spoke recklessly and that he is apologizing for speaking unguardedly. Wow, all we've heard him say so far was his short speech in Job 3. It was hard to hear, but it was understandable given all that he was experiencing. His apology for those words makes me respect his integrity even more.

How does Job describe his suffering, according to the following verses?
Job 6:4

Job 6:6-7

Job 6:11

Job 7:1-3

Job 7:4-7

Job 7:13-16

Based on your answers to the three previous questions, what do you think is the best way to handle the words of a suffering friend?

> To be a good counselor requires enormous timing, great wisdom, a long rope, and great understanding.[19]

With no acknowledgement of his suffering, Job's friends—whom he even calls his "brothers" (Job 6:15)—-attacked his integrity. Job calls them out on it and defends himself before them. We know that this was appropriate for him to do because of the background information given to us in the prologue. The Lord Himself had declared that Job was "blameless and upright, fearing God and turning from evil."

How does Job maintain his integrity and counsel his friends in the verses below?
Job 6:14

Job 6:15-21 (The "wadi" or "brook" is a seasonal stream that can become dangerously flooded, overflowing in the winter, and become completely dry in the summer, providing no refreshment.)

Job 6:22-25

Job 6:27-29

We have heard of the patience of Job. He not only endured the horrible disasters that wrecked his life, but he also endured the harsh accusations of his friends. When he had hoped that they would give him wise counsel and comfort, he became the wise man and pointed out the error of their ways.

Even though Job is responding to the words of Eliphaz, he has been addressing all three friends gathered before him. He lets them hear his words directed to the Lord as well.

What names for the Lord does Job use? Look at the references and look up the word definitions below:
Job 6:4 ______________: Strong's #7706
Hebrew word:
Hebrew definition:

Job 6:4 __________________: Strong's #433
Hebrew word:
Hebrew definition:

Job 6:10: ______________________: Strong's #6918
Hebrew word:
Hebrew definition:

Job 7:20 _______________________: Strong's #5341
Hebrew word:
Hebrew definition:

"Natsar" is used in Exodus 34:7 where the Lord is described as the One who maintains faithful love to a thousand generations, and in Psalm 31:24 where it says that He preserves the faithful. Job is upset that the Lord is watching over him, but he doesn't realize that the Lord is actually guarding him and limiting what Satan could do to him.

How would you describe Job's knowledge of the character of God?

What was the only thing that Job found comfort in, according to Job 6:10? (If you are using NKJV, it will be helpful to look at another translation.)

Beginning in Job 7:7, we hear something that sounds like prayer from him.

Please read Job 7:7-21. Highlight Job's references to **death** in one color. Highlight his references to his **misery** in one color. Highlight his **questions** to the Lord in another color.

Job 7:7-21 NLT 7O God, remember that my life is but a breath, and I will never again feel happiness. 8You see me now, but not for long. You will look for me, but I will be gone. 9Just as a cloud dissipates and vanishes, those who die will not come back. 10They are gone forever from their home -- never to be seen again. 11I cannot keep from speaking. I must express my anguish. My bitter soul must complain. 12Am I a sea monster or a dragon that you must place me under guard? 13I think, "My bed will comfort me, and sleep will ease my misery," 14but then you shatter me with dreams and terrify me with visions. 15I would rather be strangled -- rather die than suffer like this. 16I hate my life and don't want to go on living. Oh, leave me alone for my few remaining days. 17What are people, that you should make so much of us, that you should think of us so often? 18For you examine us every morning and test us every moment. 19Why won't you leave me alone, at least long enough for me to swallow! 20If I have sinned, what have I done to you, O watcher of all humanity? Why make me your target? Am I a burden to you? 21Why not just forgive my sin and take away my guilt? For soon I will lie down in the dust and die. When you look for me, I will be gone.

Job had said that he had been allotted months of futility, worthlessness (Job 7:3) and his days had no hope (Job 7:6). Now he says that his life will never have happiness again, that he will die soon and be forgotten. From his perspective, his life was meaningless. And if that was the case, then he just wanted to die.

Oh! No, Job! Your life was not worthless! Your life was not meaningless! Your life was eternally significant! Even though you couldn't see it at the time and it was incredibly painful, your life was all about God's glory!

What did Job ask of the Lord in Job 7:17-18?

Given what we know from the prologue of Job, how would you answer his question?

I think Job was the first to record that question, and then another man after God's own heart considered it as well. I think David was quoting Job in Psalm 8:4.

What is the theme of Psalm 8, according to Psalm 8:1?

What happens when the Lord is praised, according to Psalm 8:2?

What is David's attitude according to Psalm 8:3-4?

Every day *that we praise, trust, thank, and/or honor God is eternally significant. Will you make it your desire and your goal to do or say at least one thing every day that acknowledges God's glorious reputation? Even if no one else on the earth notices it, the Lord and His enemies will.*

Go ahead. Make today count for eternity! Please write a prayer of praise to our great Creator God and to His Son our Savior, Jesus Christ.

ᔓBlessed be the Name of the Lord.ᔓ

At the end of Job's speech, he asked several sincere questions as he tried to understand what was happening to him. He was spiritually confused, and he wasn't getting any answers from God. He was basically asking God to show him if there was some sin in his life that he needed to confess. This is always the right thing to do.

It was not a confession of sin, for Job still maintained his integrity; but it was an opportunity for God to deal with areas in Job's life that he knew nothing about. [20]

Lesson 10 ꟼ Job 8

SHORT BUT NOT SWEET

We are going to devote this entire lesson to the words of Bildad and his worldview. But like the spider's web that he himself will mention, his arguments are weak and collapse in light of the heavenly background to which we have been privy. Don't get tangled up in his sticky ideas.

Please pray for understanding of the Scriptures inspired by the Holy Spirit.

Bildad's speech is a response to Job's plea to the Lord: "What is man, that you make so much of him, and that you set your heart on him, visit him every morning and test him every moment? How long will you not look away from me, nor leave me alone till I swallow my spit?" Job 7:17-19 ESV

We noted in our previous lesson that Job was spiritually confused and was not getting any answers from God. His questions in the verses above indicate that he felt like the Lord had fixed His eyes on Job with the frowning and angry look of an interrogator. Job felt that the Lord was "visiting" him—examining him and testing him every moment of the day, all day long, with an unending onslaught of attacks.

How many questions does Job ask God in Job 7:7-21?

What is the first thing that Bildad says to Job? See Job 8:1-2.

> Bildad thought that his speeches were hard and rough, and stout against God, and very indecent and unbecoming a creature to his Maker. . . . They were like wind, vain and empty, great swelling words, but words of vanity; they were spoken, and seemed big, but had nothing solid and substantial in them.[21]

Uh oh. Bildad sure doesn't begin his speech with much sensitivity. "He heard Job's words with his ears, but his heart heard nothing."[22] Here comes another accusation. We will see that Bildad's exhortations, attempts at encouragement, and his explanations all completely ignore Job's feelings and real-time experiences. Bildad will confidently defend God, but he limits God as he does so. The basic problem with Bildad is that he doesn't know what he doesn't know!

Please read Job 8:1-22.

Consider the rhetorical question asked by Bildad in Job 8:3. What is the expected answer? Rewrite Job 8:3 as a statement, rather than a question.

What is Bildad's explanation for the deaths of Job's children, according to Job 8:3-4?

What is Bildad's exhortation to Job? What two actions should Job take and why would God respond, according to Job 8:5-6?

"To seek" is the Hebrew word "shachar," meaning "to be up early at any task, with the implication of earnestness, to seek diligently early in the morning." This is exactly how Job is described in the first chapter: "he would rise early in the morning and offer burnt offerings" for his children (Job 1:5). Didn't Bildad know that about his friend? He has made about five comments. He has said more than enough already.

What can we learn from Bildad's insensitivity about how to respond to a hurting friend?

What is the best thing that someone has said to you during a time of difficulty and/or grief?

Bildad advises Job according to his worldview, defending God's justice according to the "retribution principle." This basically means that the good will prosper and the bad will suffer. For Bildad, everything is black or white. Bad or good. Retribution or reward. There is no other color, not even shades of beige or brown or gray.

Bildad believes: God punishes the wicked.
All suffering is punishment for sin.
There is no other explanation.
God does not pervert justice, so Job is suffering for his sin.

What does Bildad base his belief system on, according to Job 8:8-10?

The truth about human existence, according to Bildad, is to be learned and learned from others.[23]

Yes, there is much to be learned from others. But we must turn to divine revelation for fuller understanding. And still, we must leave room for the mysteries of God.

What did Moses say in Deuteronomy 29:29? Does this cause comfort or consternation for you?

Bildad thought he knew it all. His words reveal to us that he hardly knew Job. He even implies that Job has forgotten God and is a hypocrite, at heart a godless man.

Bildad explains and defends the retribution principle with several illustrations. Summarize his points below.
Job 8:11-13: the godless are like papyrus that . . .

Job 8:13-15: the godless's confidence is like a spider web that . . .

Job 8:16-19: the godless are like a plant that . . .

How did Bildad try to encourage Job in Job 8:7 and Job 8:21-22?

Ugh! How would you feel if you were Job and heard those words? Every now and then I hear an honest reaction to empty clichés. Someone says: "Everything will be okay." And the one suffering yells: "NO IT WON'T!!!" Job certainly could have said, "Bildad, what are you talking about? My children are dead! I will never even smile again, much less laugh!"

Bildad's words of encouragement were empty, because his basic belief about Job was flawed, and Job knew it. I mentioned earlier that Bildad didn't know what he didn't know! For that, we can be sympathetic toward Bildad; but his arrogance in his ignorance is so frustrating.

The retribution principle is stated in Job 8:20. Job and his friends assumed his suffering was a result of being rejected by God. Is Job 8:20 consistent with Job 2:3? Why or why not?

Bildad's presupposition was that if God deviates from His own prescribed retribution principle, then He would be acting unjustly. This assumption leaves no room for God's ways that are higher than our ways. There must be space in our worldview for an incomprehensible God, for a supernatural being, for an unseen spiritual reality, for miracles, and for surprises. Jesus' virgin birth, Jesus' identity as the God-Man, His resurrection, forgiveness, grace, justification, the indwelling Holy Spirit, glorification, and our eternal future are all at stake if we don't allow God to color outside the lines of the picture that He drew in the first place.

Bildad does not know that to deny the universal applicability of retribution is **not** to deny the righteousness of God.[24]

If something is flawed, it must be our own beliefs and understandings, not God or His attributes or actions. It's time to look at our own ideas and beliefs.

Where do people get their ideas about life if they don't read the Bible as the Word of God?

What are some old wives' tales or fables or traditions or clichés that people live by?

Where do you get your information about God, Jesus, and the meaning of life?

There are some people who say that "if that's the way God is, then I don't want that kind of God."

What, if anything, do you find contradictory about the attributes or actions of God? Do you accept what you don't understand and what you cannot reconcile?

There are times when I am overwhelmed, distressed, grieved, or just confused. And I can't figure anything out. When I'm lost in a black hole of not understanding events, circumstances, trials, or even biblical truth, there is always one thing that I ***know:*** *Jesus loves me. Jesus loves me, this I know, for the Bible tells me so. And knowing this is enough.*

May you have the power to understand, as all God's people should, how wide, how long, how high, and how deep his love is. May you experience the love of Christ, though it is too great to understand fully. **Ephesians 3:18-19** NLT

Thank You Lord for Your blessing of ____

____

~Blessed be the Name of the Lord.~

Lesson 11 ~ Job 9 and 10

IT'S COMPLICATED

Do you enjoy the magician's trick of pulling a silk scarf out of his pocket? To cause awe and wonder among all ages, he tugs on the white scarf peeking out of his breast pocket and before you know it, you see a red scarf appearing, then a blue, and another white, then a yellow, a turquoise, another red, a green, a purple . . . and so on and so on and so on. The surprising thing is not just that the magician pulls a scarf out of his suit pocket but that he somehow has about 50 scarves tucked away in that little place!

I'd like you to keep the variety of colored scarves in mind as we study Job's third speech. He has much to say; it's multi-colored; and he certainly will bring attention to the wonders of our God. And as some magicians get flustered and frustrated when things don't go the way they've planned, so too will Job show his frustration and continued grief because of his tragic circumstances. Just don't let my reference to a magician's sleight of hand confuse you. Our God does no tricks. He is truly amazing and a God of wonders. But like a magician, he is not required to reveal how or why He does what He does.

~ Please pray for the Holy Spirit to give you understanding of God's Word. ~

Please read Job 9:1-10:22.

Let's study these chapters in living color. I suggest you read through the nine colors and categories below, then answer the questions. This exercise will probably take some time.

I have also given you some notes after the color categories, explaining some important words and phrases. There are some cross-references and questions to answer as well! You may want to look at them before studying Job 9 and 10. It's up to you.

You will see that even though Job is still suffering and is still spiritually confused at his situation, he maintains his fear of God, his reverence, his understanding of God's sovereignty, power, perfection, and transcendence.

Answer the following questions according to Job 9:1-10:22. *Please record the verse with your notes—i.e. "8:4: God is wise in heart." You can put phrases in more than one category.*

Purple signifies royalty. What statements indicate God's majesty and grandeur?

Blue in the Bible signifies deity. What statements indicate God's divinity, His transcendence, His "God-ness"?

Orange (by my definition!) indicates something out of the ordinary, the supernatural, miracles. What statements refer to God's miraculous power?

Gray can indicate intelligence and seriousness. Job uses the language of a legal trial in these chapters. How does he express that he wants to appear in court, present his case before God, and prove his innocence? (Look for words like: dispute, answer, argue, judge.)

White indicates purity. What statements refer to God's righteousness or Job's righteousness?

Red often depicts anger. What statements refer to the anger of God or the anger of Job?

Please reflect on the "anger of God." Is God angry with Job? Why or why not?

Black can indicate depression, morbidity, and death. What statements refer to Job's suffering and/or anticipation of death?

Yellow flowers usually represent friendship, but the color yellow can also represent conflict. What statements show that Job wants reconciliation and resolution with God?

Green can indicate harmony and optimism. Do you see any statements reflecting this?

For clarification of some hard to understand words and phrases, I have given you some explanations below, other scriptures to consider, and a few more questions to answer!

Job 9:2 *– Job says,* ***"Truly I know it is so."*** *He is actually agreeing with Bildad's doctrine of retribution, that the wicked suffer and the righteous are rewarded. The problem is that Job is suffering even though he is blameless and upright. The square peg of this doctrine is not fitting into the round hole of his experience.*

Job 9:11 *– Job* ***cannot see*** *or* ***perceive*** *God passing by although he can see the evidence of His existence. God is omnipresent, but invisible, spirit, and incomprehensible.*

Job 9:13 *– What is* ***Rahab*** *doing here?! It's not the woman from Jericho who hid the Israelite spies. The Hebrew noun "rahab" means pride, arrogance. In this verse and a few other Scriptures, it refers to a sea monster, perhaps the same one as Leviathan in Job 3:8 and Job 7:12.*

Job 9:18; Job 10:1 *– Job expresses his* ***bitterness.*** *This is the Hebrew word "mar," related to "maror"—the bitter herb eaten at Passover to denote the hard suffering of the Israelites in Egypt (Exodus 1:14, 12:8). It is also related to the name Naomi used for herself: "Mara"—bitter because of the way the Lord had dealt with her (Ruth 1:20). The word is also related to "myrrh"—an ointment used for embalming and the gift given at Christ's birth representing His suffering (Matthew 2:11, John 19:39). The Hebrew root word and those related to it appear in the book of Job 10 times, more than in any other Old Testament book.*

Job constantly experienced bitterness, the emotional response to his tragic, heart-crushing situation. It was a dark, painful, gloominess, which allowed no light of hope. I googled the word "gloom" and came across a game by the same name. Its description is appropriate for Job: "The world of Gloom is a sad and benighted place. The sky is gray, the tea is cold, and a new tragedy lies around every corner. Debt, disease, heartache, and packs of rabid flesh-eating mice—just when it seems like things can't get any worse, they do." Sadly for Job, it was no make-believe game.

Job 9:20 –"my own mouth would condemn me." *Job believed that if he stood before God in court, in the presence of Almighty God, he would become so disoriented and tongue-tied that he would end up testifying against himself.*

What would you say if you stood face to face with the Lord God on High?

Job 9:22 – "It is all one thing." *Some translations say "it's all the same." Job felt that it didn't matter whether he was innocent or guilty, that God would punish him. This was definitely a distortion of truth brought about by his anguish. "Both the righteous and wicked do die by God's sovereign decree, but their destinies are different. In the end God rewards the righteous and punishes the wicked."* [25]

Job 9:23 *– Again, Job's despair distorted his thinking. God does not* **mock** *the innocent. Job felt that God was enjoying watching his suffering and that God was just standing by and doing nothing.*

Job knew that his suffering was not a direct result of sin in his life, but sometimes we do suffer because of our own sin or the consequences of others' sins. There are biblical truths that we must depend on whatever the reason for our trials.

What does Psalm 56:8 tell us about God's care for us during our times of suffering?

What is the truth in Psalm 40:11-12 that we must remember and cling to when it seems that God is silent and distant?

What is our hope according to Lamentations 3:29-33 and Hebrews 12:10?

Job 10:4-5 *– These two verses emphasize that God is not a man with the limitations of understanding such as his friends had.*

Job 10:8-12 *– These verses beautifully and poetically describe Job's understanding that God created him. As Genesis 2:7 teaches, he says that he was made from the dust of the earth. He also refers to the time of his conception and development in his mother's womb as being* **"poured out like milk"** *and* **"curdled like cheese."** *These verses show that human life begins at the time that the sperm of a man (referred to as "milk"), fertilizes the egg of a woman (referred to as "curdling"), and that human life is formed by the very hands of God. Another beautiful description of the creation of each person is described in Psalm 139:14-16, and it corresponds perfectly with Job's statements.*

What biblical truths should we remember and delight in according to Job 10:8-12 and Psalm 139:14-17?

After having contemplated the struggles of Job expressed in chapters 9 and 10, I think it would be most encouraging to us to end our lesson today reflecting on the tender truth that the Lord created us with His own hands and knows us intimately.

When I was a little girl, my grandmother used to ask me, "who's so precious?" And she loved my answer as I just repeated what she said, "so precious." That is just what you and I are to the Lord: "so precious." So very precious.

Thank You Lord for Your blessing of ______________________________________

____

Blessed be the Name of the Lord.

Lesson 12 Job 11

ZOPHAR SPEAKS

Hello there friend! I'd like to introduce Mr. Zophar to you. I think his name is fascinating, probably just because it begins with the letter Z. I remember learning how to write my own name, and my first grade teacher told me that I would be learning the last letter of the alphabet before anyone else! There's just something out of the ordinary about the letter Z!

What will we find out of the ordinary with Zophar? He is brutally blunt, the first of the friends to come right out and accuse Job of sin. He is devoid of compassion, completely ignoring Job's misery. And Zophar is absolutely confident regarding his knowledge of God's justice. He pridefully believes that he understands the secrets of the wisdom of the Lord and challenges Job to try to grasp how God is dealing with him.

The strangest thing about Zophar is that he accurately declares truth about the Lord. He just doesn't have an accurate assessment of Job's situation. He couldn't. Job's suffering was a mystery. Even now that we know the story behind his suffering, we can't fully explain the mystery of God's ways.

Zophar shows us how wrong someone who is right can be. He is a portrait of pride. Let's learn from his mistakes.

ல **Please pray for understanding of the Scriptures inspired by the Holy Spirit.** ல

Please read Job 11:1-20.

What does Zophar think about the words of Job, according to Job 11:1-4?

What do you think? Should a multitude of words always be answered?

Zophar considered Job's words pure mockery (vv.2-3), for he thought Job was claiming flawless doctrine and sinless perfection (v.4). Job has steadfastly maintained his innocence or blamelessness in contrast with wickedness (9:22), but he did not claim to be perfect (7:21). Though he complained bitterly of the treatment God appeared to be giving him, to this point he has not been particularly sarcastic nor has he mocked God or even ridiculed his friends. He has accused them of being shallow in their arguments and callous in the way they have dealt with him (6:24-27).[26]

What does Zophar want Job to know, according to Job 11:5-6? (It would be helpful to look at several translations to understand these verses.)

This is the bottom line assessment of Zophar: Job is a sinner who is being punished by God and being punished far less than he deserves. This is judgmental and heartless.

How does Zophar rebuke Job and challenge his understanding of the wisdom of God? See Job 11:7-12.

All this was designed to humble Job, but Zophar apparently doubted that it would. He then attempted heavy handed shock treatment to get through to Job. The sharpness of his sarcasm is demonstrated in v.12. Zophar labeled Job a witless, empty-headed man with as much chance to become wise as a wild donkey has to be born tame.[27]

I am sad to say that I myself have had the attitude of Zophar quite a few times: that I know it all, that I have all the answers and my friend is clueless to the truth, and that they just need to open their eyes to the error of their ways.

What about you? Do you ever act or think like a "know-it-all"? Have you had an experience where you thought that you had all the right, biblical answers?

It is so prideful to think that we know all about God, all about His ways, and all about His purposes. Even with all of the biblical revelation that we have, we don't always have an explanation for a situation.

What do the following verses teach us?
Ecclesiastes 3:11

Isaiah 40:8

Romans 11:33

What is the surprising and comforting truth given to us in 1 Corinthians 2:7-12?

The only way you can know about God is what He is pleased to reveal of Himself to us. I have come to the conclusion that He has revealed very little of Himself to us. In fact, the little that He has revealed to us has some of us so awestruck and some so confused that we can see why He hasn't revealed more of Himself to us.[28]

How great is our God! His greatness is unsearchable! He is infinitely beyond our comprehension!

It takes dependence on the Holy Spirit and humility and an accurate assessment of myself to correctly fear God. He is God and I am not. I cannot fear Him on my own terms. I think it is helpful to think of our Lord as C.S. Lewis illustrated Him —as Aslan the Lion.

"Aslan is a lion—the Lion, the great Lion." "Ooh" said Susan. "I'd thought he was a man. Is he—quite safe? I shall feel rather nervous about meeting a lion . . . ." "Safe?" said Mr. Beaver . . . . "Who said anything about safe? 'Course he isn't safe. But he's good. He's the King, I tell you." [29]

I agree with Mr. Beaver. God isn't safe. He will allow us to experience pain and suffering. And God is good. He will be with us every step of that suffering.

The Son of God, who was God Himself, even experienced pain and suffering. And that to a degree greater than any human ever has or ever will experience it.

Please read John 12:23-28. What were the purposes of Christ's suffering and His death, according to these verses?

The disciples didn't understand why Jesus had to die, any more than Job's friends understood why he was suffering. But God knew His good purposes. Ultimately, His glory was at stake in both Job's and Jesus' lives. Let's not forget that Satan wanted to dishonor and discredit God. Satan may have listened with anticipation as Zophar presented an option for Job to bargain his way out of his misery.

What did Zophar tell Job to do and what would he receive, according to Job 11:13-19?

This false solution, repentance, was based upon the false assumption that Job was under the discipline of God for his sin . . . . If Job had repented, it would have demonstrated that his obedience was truly based on God's blessings, rather than his unwavering trust in God in spite of the circumstances.[30]

What was the final nail on the coffin of Zophar's brutal counsel? How did he view Job and what did he think would happen to Job if he did not repent, according to Job 11:20?

The temptation in Zophar's counsel was to pursue prosperity, rather than to place all trust in the Lord. At first, it seems that his instruction for Job to repent of his sins is appropriate. If you believe the Bible, then you believe that all men have sinned and fall short of the glory of God (Romans 3:23). But Zophar's instruction was based on the wrong assessment of Job's suffering. We know that Job was not suffering because of his sin. Job knew that he wasn't suffering because of his sin. Therefore, the only appropriate action on Job's part was for him to trust God through his misery.

Prosperity and a life free from suffering is something we all want, to one degree or another. Have you ever been tempted to take a short cut from trusting God and get on the fast track to "the good life"? How might you put your trust in something other than the Lord when waiting for relief from your circumstances or when pursuing a desire?

Let's train ourselves to turn to the Lord and trust Him during life's best and worst times.

Thank You Lord for Your blessing of ____

____

Blessed be the Name of the Lord.

Lesson 13 ~ Job 12, 13 and 14

WISDOM, INTEGRITY, AND HOPE

You may not have realized it, but you are on the sidelines of an intellectual competition between Job and his friends. It's a little like a debate. Job and his friends present their arguments as eloquent orators and make their points through rhetorical questions and powerful declarations. In the middle of Job's misery, these men are having a battle of the brains. In today's culture we have sports play-offs, cook-offs, sing-offs, dance-offs, and more! In the book of Job, we have a "speak-off"!

I thought a "speak-off" was my own original idea . . . but it actually exists: "Washburn University's Communication Department hosts the bi-annual Nall Speak Off Competition. The Nall Speak Off is an informative speaking contest, comprised of beginning students from the various Public Speaking sections being offered during the semester." [31]

If you look back at our outline of the book of Job in Lesson 7, page 33, you will see that we are at the concluding speech of Round One of the Speak-off between Job and his friends. Job was either given extra time or just went way over his allotted time, because the speech we are about to study is the longest so far. In the next three chapters, Job gives his rebuttal to Zophar.

Zophar's points had been:

1. *Job was a guilty sinner (11:1-4)*
2. *Job had no knowledge of God (Job 11:5-12)*
3. *Job would have hope if he would repent (Job 11:13-20)*

Job will respond to each point, but not in the same order as above.[32]

1. *Response to Zophar's point #2: He has wisdom and understanding of God just as his friends (Job 12)*
2. *Response to Zophar's point #1: He affirmed his integrity (Job 13)*
3. *Response to Zophar's point #3: He declares that his hope is almost gone and death is near (Job 14)*

~ Please pray for the Holy Spirit to give you understanding of God's Word. ~

Please read Job 12, 13, and 14.

How does Job defend himself in Job 12:1-4?

What evidence does Job give in Job 12:6 to show that his suffering is not due to his sin?

What does Job want his friends to understand, that even all creation understands, according to Job 12:7-10?

Job's strong, God-centered theology gave him a perspective which accepted from God both good and bad. [33]

Job has been trying to make his friends understand that sometimes the wicked do prosper and the blameless do suffer. And God is sovereignly in control over all of it. He then quotes what one commentator says is a "hymn to the power of God in the human world," and it presents "many examples of the theme of the reversal of fortunes."[34]

How is God praised in the hymn in Job 12:13-25? What is one example of a reversal of fortunes?

And what is Job's perspective on God's power, according to Job 13:1?

When a crisis comes into your life, what do you say about God?

Now that we have considered Job's understanding and trust of God's sovereignty, it's a good time to reflect on something incredible in this chapter.

What does Job 12:9 say?

This verse contains the only occurrence out of the mouth of Job or his friends of the most personal and most mysterious name of the Lord. (It is used by the narrator in the prologue and epilogue, but only used in the speeches here.)

Please look up the definition for the following word:
LORD: Strong's #3068
Hebrew word:
Hebrew definition:

This is the "glorious and awesome name" of the Lord (Deut. 28:58). It refers to God's underived self-existence and also indicates His eternality, autonomy, independence, and unchangeable-ness. As I mentioned previously, it is His most personal name, indicating that He is a God in relationship with and near to His people.

Why is it appropriate for Job to refer to God as Yahweh at this time in his speech?

What does Job desire, according to Job 13:3?

He doesn't want to talk about his situation with his friends anymore. They haven't been any help; they have only added misery to his misery. Job wants to talk to God.

Job 13:4-13 contains Job's rebuke to his friends regarding their representation of God, specifically their presumption to speak for God and declare Job a sinner. In these verses, how does Job describe the words of his friends; and what does he want from them?

He keeps it no secret that he thinks they are totally out of line! The Jewish Study Bible translates Job 13:4 with Job saying: "all of you are quacks."[35] *And Job pleads with his friends—just be quiet! —so that he can talk directly with God. He is ready to risk his life and go before God . . . "come what may." (Job 13:13) That's a phrase that is attributed to Shakespeare (in Macbeth), and old French (vaille que vaille) and old Spanish (que sera sera). We see here however that it originated in one of the oldest writings of all!*

Job makes one more declaration to his friends.

What does he say he will do, according to Job 13:14-19?

One of the most well-known verses from Job's mouth is found in Job 13:15. I have considered it many times as a statement of faith. It is. But I have not understood it in context before now.

Please write out Job 13:15.

I have always thought that Job meant that even though God had allowed all these tragedies and his nearly fatal disease and even if God were to take Job's life, he would still trust Him. That's not what his statement means.

Remember that the context of Job's statement was his desire to speak to God. He wanted to be face to face with God and talk about his situation. Even if God were to "slay him" in His holy presence, Job was saying that he would still hope for God to vindicate him.

Job was so certain that God would receive him in His presence as one who was blameless, that he was willing to stake his life on it. With that confidence, he concluded his comments to his friends. In our next lesson we will look at the comments he directed to the Lord.

At this point, Job was just on the brink of self-righteousness and arrogance before God. Let's close our lesson with a humble prayer offered by the psalmist David, who recognized that his hope and praise was in the righteousness of God alone.

Psalm 71:12-16 NAS

[12] O God, do not be far from me; O my God, hasten to my help!
[13] Let those who are adversaries of my soul be ashamed and consumed;
Let them be covered with reproach and dishonor, who seek to injure me.
[14] But as for me, I will hope continually, and will praise Thee yet more and more.
[15] My mouth shall tell of Thy righteousness,
And of Thy salvation all day long; for I do not know the sum of them.
[16] I will come with the mighty deeds of the Lord God;
I will make mention of Thy righteousness, Thine alone.

Thank You Lord for Your blessing of ____

____

~Blessed be the Name of the Lord.~

Lesson 14 ~ Job 14

WHAT HE WOULD SAY TO GOD

Do you remember that Job used the language of a legal trial and longed to appear in court to present his case before God? This began in Job 9 and 10 and continued in Job 12-14. We took a short recess from the court trial that Job initiated. The last thing that he said to his friends was, "Can anyone bring charges against me? If so, I will be silent and die." Job 13:19 NIV

Job has "prepared his case" (v.18) and is sure that he will win . . . . Job is asking God to meet him in court so they can talk over God's "case" against Job and Job's "case" against God. [36]

Let's review what has been said and allow Job to resume his presentation.

ᔓ Please pray for understanding of the Scriptures inspired by the Holy Spirit. ᔓ

Please read Job 12:1-14:22.

What two things does Job ask of God, in Job 13:21?

Does Job 13:22 indicate that God has responded to Job or not?

What does he want to know, according to Job 13:23?

Even though Job has repeatedly declared his blamelessness, he now asks God to tell him how many sins he has committed. His perspective on his suffering is being swayed by the accusations of his friends. He even wonders if he is being punished for sins he committed in his youth. The rest of his comments will show us that he feels like he is on death row, awaiting the end of his life, with almost no hope for release from God's imprisonment.

According to Job 14:1, what does Job say that all mankind experiences? How does this support his own declaration that he is not suffering because of his sin?

In Job 14 below and on the next page, using 5 different colors, please highlight words and phrases that refer to the following topics:
1 –the brevity of life 2 –the sovereignty of God 3 –death 4 –life after death 5 –hope

Job 14:1-22 ESV Man who is born of a woman is few of days and full of trouble. [2]He comes out like a flower and withers; he flees like a shadow and continues not. [3]And do You open Your eyes on such a one and bring me into judgment with You? [4]Who can bring a clean thing out of an unclean? There is not one. [5]Since his days are determined, and the number of his months is with You, and You have appointed his limits that he cannot pass, [6]look away from him and leave him alone, that he may enjoy, like a hired hand, his day. [7]For there is hope for a tree, if it be cut down, that it will sprout again, and that its shoots will not cease. [8]Though its root grow old in the earth, and its stump die in the soil, [9]yet at the scent of water it will bud and put out branches like a young plant. [10]But a man dies and is laid low; man breathes his last, and where is he? [11]As waters fail from a lake and a river wastes away and dries up, [12]so a man lies down and rises not again; till the heavens are no more he will not awake or be roused out of his sleep. [13]Oh that You would hide me in Sheol, that You would conceal me until Your wrath be past, that You would appoint me a set time, and remember me! [14]If a man dies, shall he live again? All the days of my service I would wait, till my renewal should come. [15]You would call, and I would answer You; You would long for the work of Your hands. [16]For then You would number my steps; You would not keep watch over my sin; [17]my transgression would be sealed up in a bag, and You would cover over my iniquity. [18]But the mountain falls and crumbles away, and the rock is removed from its place; [19]the waters wear away the stones; the torrents wash away the soil of the earth; so You destroy the hope of man. [20]You prevail forever against him, and he passes; You change his countenance, and send him away. [21]His sons come to honor, and he does not know it; they are brought low, and he perceives it not. [22]He feels only the pain of his own body, and he mourns only for himself.

What is Job's perspective on the length of life?

What did Job believe about the sovereignty of God and the length of man's life? What impact does this have on your perspective about the length of your own life?

When Job said, "till the heavens are no more he will not awake or be roused out of his sleep" (Job 14:12), he seemed to understand that it would take divine intervention to make a man rise from the dead.

Note from the following passages what God did or what He will do that changes everything!
Psalm 102:25-27

Isaiah 51:6

Isaiah 65:17

Matthew 28:2-7

2 Peter 3:7-14

Revelation 20:11-21:1

Job 14:13-15 indicates a hope for life after death. What did Job want from God?

The Hebrew word *Sheol* appears nearly seventy times in the Old Testament. Much of the confusion about it comes from the fact that, at times, it is translated "hell," and other times, "the grave." Sheol is not hell, and though the word can refer to the grave, it is not the grave, either. Sheol is a holding place where departed spirits await their final judgment. The grave is the place where the body is laid. Sheol is the place where the spirit of the deceased is living—as alive as ever. (Isaiah 14:9; Psalm 49:14-15; Luke 16:22-26; 2 Peter 2:9) [37]

Will you spend time in Sheol? When your spirit no longer resides in your mortal body, where will it be? Answer your question based on 2 Corinthians 5:5-8. According to these verses, what guarantees your destination?

In Job 14:14, Job talked about waiting through the days of his difficult service until his renewal would come. The Hebrew word for renewal—"khalapi"—is also translated as relief or change. Job did not have an understanding of life after death, and he longed to know "if a man dies, will he live again?"

What did Jesus say in John 11:25?

What did Paul explain about life after death and the change that those who trust in Christ will receive? Note your answers from the verses below.

1 Corinthians 15:3-4

1 Corinthians 15:12

1 Corinthians 15:20-22

1 Corinthians 15:51-57

There's a reason we sing about victory in Jesus! What a relief to know that one day, the troubles of this life will be over, we will be in the presence of the Lord, and we will be clothed in immortality! We have so much to hope for!

Job wanted to hope for something. But God did not reveal His plans at that time.

How did Job describe his hope in Job 14:18-22?

> In his depression Job saw only God's oppressive might and the prospect of a painful future calamity followed by a dismal state of death. [38]

Job could not see past his present suffering. If there was life after death, he could endure his suffering; but he didn't know if there was any existence beyond the grave.

How do the promises of God's Word enable you to fight discouragement, hopelessness, and depression?

Steven Lawson considers the lessons learned from Job 14 and makes the following points:[39]

1. *All suffering is temporal. No matter how painful the ordeal we are undergoing, it will eventually pass.*
2. *All suffering is useful. Suffering is never needless but always with divine design.*
3. *All suffering is Christlike. Human pain identifies us with Christ, who knew adversity in this world. He lived with the cross before Him and suffered under the most grueling death imaginable. As we undergo trials, we are actually being drawn closer to Christ, our suffering Savior.*

Job wanted an audience with God, and we've heard what he would say to Him.

What has this lesson prompted you to want to say to the Lord? Record your prayer to Him, and remember to thank Him for at least one thing.

Thank You Lord for Your blessing of ____

____

Blessed be the Name of the Lord.

Lesson 15 ∾ Job 15

WISDOM FROM THE OH-SO WISE ELIPHAZ

I've got good news and bad news. Which do you want first? Hope you said good news! It's time to welcome Job's very experienced friend Eliphaz back to the podium. The good news is that he has been the gentlest speaker of the three friends. The bad news is that in Job 15, he is no longer Mr. Nice Guy. But the good news about him is that he speaks truth. The bad news, however, is that the truth is misapplied. There's more good news—Eliphaz pretty much says the same thing that he said the first time, so it's fairly easy to understand. And even more good news . . . his second speech is shorter than his first!

∾ Please pray for the Holy Spirit to give you understanding of God's Word. ∾

Please review the perspective of Eliphaz. Read Job 4:1-5:27.

What stands out to you about his first speech at this point in our study?

Now please read the first speech in the second round of the dialogues between Job and his friends. (Did that confuse you? Check out the outline on page 33) Read Job 15:1-35.

With his rhetorical opening questions in Job 15:1-3, how does Eliphaz describe Job's comments?

How would you say it in today's language?

Job 15:4-6 bluntly expresses Eliphaz's accusation against Job. Summarize this in your own words.

I just shake my head sometimes as I read what these friends said to Job. We remember from the prologue the description of Job as a man who feared God and regularly rose early in the morning to offer burnt offerings for his children. But Eliphaz thinks all of Job's piety is just an act covering up his secret sins. He also indicates that the words coming out of Job's mouth are a result of his sinful state and they are self-incriminating.

How does Eliphaz belittle Job's wisdom and preserve his own superiority, according to Job 15:7-12?

The book of Job has been described as one full of irony, and that is so obvious in Job 15:8! "Were you listening at God's secret council? Do you have a monopoly on wisdom?" NLT *Wouldn't you like to ask Eliphaz those questions?! He's the one who talked as if he knew everything there was to know. But we actually were allowed to hear the private conversation between God and Satan.*

How does your awareness of the "behind-the-scenes story" of Job affect your assessment of circumstances in your life or your friend's lives?

It's time to look at the key perspective that dictates everything that Eliphaz thinks and says. His worldview is expressed in Job 15:14-16 when he challenges Job's claim of blamelessness. This statement is based on his terrifying experience of visions in the night, which he described in Job 4:17-19.

What was Eliphaz's worldview, based on Job 15:14-17?

He did speak the truth about the nature of man, about the status of angels, and about the condition of the heavens. That was good. But he stated that truth to explain his perspective that Job was suffering due to his depravity. That was bad. He was wrong.

In spite of the fact that Eliphaz was way off base regarding the reason for Job's suffering, his first question is worth pondering.

Job 15:14a: What is man, that he could be pure?

This question is one of the most basic, most important questions since the creation of Adam. Is man basically good or bad? Let's start back at the beginning.

What does Genesis 1:27 and 31 tell you about man?

In the earliest days of the creation of man, life was good! Adam and Eve knew who God was and who they were. All creation enjoyed purity and goodness. Augustine described Adam's status at that time as both "able to sin" and "able to not sin." That means he had a choice.

What choice did Adam and Eve both make, according to Genesis 3:9-12?

After they made their choice (which I believe every single human being would also have made), they became "not able to not sin" as well as remaining "able to sin." Romans 6:5-17 explains that every person is a slave to sin before being freed from that slavery through belief in Jesus Christ.

So the answer to—"what is man, that he could be pure?"—is that man is a creation of God and unable to be pure by his own ability. Eliphaz was expressing the truth about the nature of man.

<u>Job 15:14b: And he who is born of a woman, that he could be righteous?</u>

The poetry of Eliphaz presents this question in parallel to the first one. It basically asks the same thing. Can any man ever be born who is perfectly innocent before God? This is a wonderful question to ask! These two questions posed by Eliphaz are possibly the best two questions that every person who ever lived on Planet Earth could ask!

Can a person be pure in the eyes of God? No. Not by his own ability.

Can anyone ever be born who could be righteous? Humanly speaking, no. But miraculously, yes!

What do the following verses tell you?
Galatians 4:4-7

Matthew 1:21-25

1 John 3:5

Eliphaz did speak truth as he pointed out that no human being can be pure in the sight of God. He made that point, however, to explain that Job's suffering was due to his sin. This was truth misapplied.

At the same time, without knowing it, he proposed a situation that no one would have thought possible. And many throughout history have thought it to be impossible. Jesus, the man born of a woman, was sinless. He was "not able to sin" because He was God in the flesh. What a mystery! But what a miracle that makes a way for a man to be saved from being a slave to sin and saved from eternal pain.

How are the futures of the wicked and the righteous described in Psalm 1:5-6 and John 5:28-29?

The rest of what Eliphaz has to say to Job is a "dramatic description of the dreadful fate of the wicked."[40] *Once again, there is truth to what he says; it just isn't true for Job, although Eliphaz makes references to the disasters that Job has experienced.*

Please read Job 15:20-35.

What will the wicked experience?

Why will they experience this?

Eliphaz insinuated that Job, as a wicked man, had experienced what he deserved. Note the parallels between the phrases below and Job 1:13-22 and Job 2:7-8.

Job 15	Job 1:13-22, Job 2:7-8
Job 15:20: the wicked man writhes in pain all his days	____________________
Job 15:21: dreadful sounds are in his ears	____________________
Job 15:21: in prosperity the destroyer comes upon him	____________________
Job 15:22: a sword is waiting for him	____________________
Job 15:28: his houses are crumbling to rubble	____________________
Job 15:29: he will no longer be rich	____________________
Job 15:34: the godless will be barren	____________________
Job 15:34: fire consumes the tents of bribery	____________________

In his closing words (vv.34-35), Eliphaz gave the hardest blow of all: he called Job a hypocrite and a godless man, and he blamed him for the tragedies that had befallen him and his family. Job had secretly "conceived" sin, and now sin had given birth to suffering and death.[41]

I'd say that brings us back to the bad news about Eliphaz. He was right and he was wrong. Even his perspective about the fate of the wicked wasn't all accurate. Some wicked people are as happy as can be, and incredibly successful and wealthy.

The following scene from the movie God's Not Dead *describes what can happen sometimes:*

Mark: You prayed and believed your whole life. Never done anything wrong. And here you are. You're the nicest person I know. I am the meanest. You have dementia. My life is perfect. Explain that to me!
Mark's Mother: Sometimes the devil allows people to live a life free of trouble because he doesn't want them turning to God. Their sin is like a jail cell, except it is all nice and comfy and there doesn't seem to be any reason to leave. The door's wide open. Till one day, time runs out, and the cell door slams shut, and suddenly it's too late. [42]

What is the hope for sinners, according to 2 Peter 3:9 and Romans 2:4?

Take all the good news and bad news that we've considered today to heart. Let's deal with bad news first this time, then end on a good note.

In your opinion, what was the worst bad news you learned about in the study today?

From your own perspective, what was the best good news from today's lesson?

God is good. All the time. All the time. God is good.

Blessed be the Name of the Lord.

Lesson 16 ➰ Job 16 and 17

AN ANCHOR IN THE STORM

How do you feel about boating? Are you a seafarer or a landlubber? Both grandfathers on my husband's side owned cabin cruisers, so there is salt water running through the veins of his family! I, on the other hand, have a serious tendency towards seasickness. But give me some motion-sickness medicine, and I'll go along for a ride. The smoother the better.

I've learned that you never sail away without an anchor, and it is critical to set the anchor firmly in the seabed to keep your boat from drifting away or crashing into another boat. And just because your boat is anchored doesn't mean that it will be a resting place without turbulence.

Job's life right now is like a boat that is being tossed up and down by stormy waves. It's rough. He has anchored himself in the Lord, but he is still experiencing extreme chaos as the sea of life is roiling beneath him.

➰ Please pray for understanding of the Scriptures inspired by the Holy Spirit. ➰

Please read Job 16:1 – 17:16.

What have you been thinking about Job's friends . . . and what did Job finally say to them in the first 3 verses of his speech?

And then what did Job say, in Job 16:4-5? Based on this, what is the lesson that we learn from Job regarding how we should try to comfort others?

Let's look at a few more comments that Job made about his friends, and then we will focus the remainder of our study on his distress and desire for deliverance.

According to Job 17:2-5:
How did Job describe his friends?

What was his perspective on their assumptions about him?

What did he think would be the consequences for their attitudes?

Where there is not the tenderness of a man one may question whether there be the understanding of a man. [43]

In the midst of Job's rightful frustration with his friends, he asks God to "lay down a pledge for him." (Job 17:3) He knows that only God will defend him and prove him right. None of his friends will.

Job is all alone. No one understands his grief and pain, not even his wife. Not only has he lost his business, his income, his investments, his possessions, his staff, his home, his children, and his health . . . that was more than enough to bear . . . through no fault of his own, he has also lost the respect of the community. His friends see him as a hypocrite and the world's worst sinner. His friends are even telling him that he ***deserved*** *everything that had happened to him. That makes me want to cry in anguish with him. It's outrageous.*

Now I would like for you to consider Job's suffering and compare it to the suffering of Jesus Christ. Job 16-17 has many descriptions of suffering that Christ Himself experienced.

Job was a "type" of Christ. "Typology" in the Old Testament is when a person, event, or even an object is an example of the actual person or event to come in the future. The blameless man Job, who suffered for the sake of the glory of the Lord was a foreshadowing of the sinless man Jesus, who suffered for the sake of the glory of the Lord and to save us from our sins.

Job, thus slandered by Satan, was a type of Christ, the first prophecy of whom was, that Satan should bruise his heel, and be foiled. (Genesis 3:15)[44]

With this in mind, please read Job 16:6-17:9.

I think the chart on the next two pages will be the best way to compare and capture the similarities between the suffering of Job and Jesus. Make notes of what Jesus experienced in the chart. Please don't let the structure of this exercise diminish the emotion that you may feel as you consider what Jesus endured for the glory of His Father and for your salvation.

Job's Suffering	Jesus' Suffering
[6] Even if I speak, my suffering is not relieved, and if I hold back, what have I lost?	**Matthew 26:36-39**
[7] Surely He has now exhausted me. You have devastated my entire family.	**Matthew 26:55-57**
[8] You have shriveled me up-- it has become a witness; My frailty rises up against me and testifies to my face.	**John 19:1-3, Isaiah 53:3-4**
[9] His anger tears at me, and He harasses me. He gnashes His teeth at me. My enemy pierces me with His eyes.	**Matthew 26:31, Zechariah 13:7, Isaiah 53:10**
[10] They open their mouths against me and strike my cheeks with contempt; they join themselves together against me.	**Matthew 27:27-30, Luke 23:10-12, John 18:19-23**
[11] God hands me over to unjust men; He throws me into the hands of the wicked.	**John 19:6-16, Acts 4:24-28**
[12] I was at ease, but He shattered me; He seized me by the scruff of the neck and smashed me to pieces. He set me up as His target;	**Luke 18:31-33**
[13] His archers surround me. He pierces my kidneys without mercy and pours my bile on the ground. [14] He breaks through my defenses again and again; He charges at me like a warrior.	**Matthew 27:22-23, John 19:33-34, Romans 8:32**
[15] I have sewn sackcloth over my skin; I have buried my strength in the dust.	**Psalm 22:15**
[16] My face has grown red with weeping, and the shadow of death covers my eyes,	**Mark 14:33-36, John 12:27, 32-33**
[17] although my hands are free from violence and my prayer is pure.	**Luke 23:3-4, 41, 47**
[18] Earth, do not cover my blood; may my cry for help find no resting place. [19] Even now my witness is in heaven, and my advocate is in the heights!	**Matthew 26:62-64**

Job's Suffering	Jesus' Suffering
[20] My friends scoff at me as I weep before God.	**Matthew 26:73-75, Mark 15:29-33**
[21] I wish that someone might arbitrate between a man and God just as a man pleads for his friend.	**Luke 23:33-35, 42-43**
Job 17:1 My spirit is broken. My days are extinguished. A graveyard awaits me.	**Matthew 26:2, 27:58-60, John 13:1**
[2] Surely mockers surround me and my eyes must gaze at their rebellion.	**Luke 23:35-39**
[3] Make arrangements! Put up security for me. Who else will be my sponsor?	**Matthew 26:53-54**
[4] You have closed their minds to understanding, therefore You will not honor them.	**Matthew 16:21-23, Mark 9:31-32**
[5] If a man informs on his friends for a price, the eyes of his children will fail.	**Matthew 26:59-60**
[6] He has made me an object of scorn to the people; I have become a man people spit at.	**Matthew 26:65-67**
[7] My eyes have grown dim from grief, and my whole body has become but a shadow.	**Luke 22:44, Psalm 22:17, Isaiah 52:14**
[8] The upright are appalled at this, and the innocent are roused against the godless.	**Luke 23:47-48**
[9] Yet the righteous person will hold to his way, and the one whose hands are clean will grow stronger.	**John 18:4-11, Mark 15:3-5, Luke 23:46**

Please summarize, in your own words, how the suffering of Job was a foreshadowing of the suffering of Christ.

We need to spend more time considering the suffering of Job and the suffering of Jesus. We will continue our study in Lesson 17, Part Two of The Anchor in the Storm.

Thank You Lord for Your blessing of ____

____

~Blessed be the Name of the Lord.~

Lesson 17 ~ Job 16 and 17

AN ANCHOR IN THE STORM: PART TWO

Please review the chart of Job's suffering and Jesus' suffering and then continue with the lesson.

~ Please pray for the Holy Spirit to give you understanding of God's Word. ~

While the extent of Job's suffering was overwhelming, the magnitude of the suffering of Christ was inconceivable. There is no way to comprehend His pain because we cannot put ourselves in His place. However, God has revealed important descriptions of His experience so that we might respond in humility and thankfulness to Him.

You may be very familiar with the truths you will see in the verses below. Please use this exercise as a reminder of what Jesus sacrificed for you and worship Him as you make your notes.

What did Jesus say about Himself in Matthew 20:28?

What did the disciple John explain in John 1:1 and 14?

What happened to Jesus and why, according to Galatians 3:13?

What does Philippians 2:5-8 tell you?

What did Jesus do, according to 2 Corinthians 8:9?

What did the only sinless man ever to live on this earth do, according to 1 Peter 2:24?

As terribly as Job suffered, who suffered more? Job or Jesus? As terribly as you may suffer, will you ever suffer as Jesus did? How can this perspective help you during extreme trials?

Now I would like to take you back to something that Job said that he most likely didn't realize had eternal significance for all men. Job's request was the same request that every man and woman on earth must make if they want to live happily ever after.

Remember that Job's speech is Hebrew poetry. I've structured the phrases according to its Hebrew punctuation. In my opinion, the ESV gives the closest translation to the original language.

Job 16:19-21 ESV

[19] Even now, behold, my witness is in heaven,
and he who testifies for me is on high.
[20] My friends scorn me;
my eye pours out tears to God,
[21] that He would argue the case of a man with God,
as a son of man does with his neighbor.

What does Job want his "witness" do for him, based on verse 19 and verse 21?

Based on these verses only, who is "he" at the beginning of verse 21? What is the antecedent of that pronoun? There are two possibilities—note them both.

How is Job's witness described in the second half of verse 21?

*Is anything surprising you? I've just seen Jesus—the Son of man! Job was asking God to testify for his sake as if He were a man testifying for the sake of another man. He was asking God to **act** like a man, but he didn't know that one day God would **become** a man!*

Here is what the Jamieson, Fausset, and Brown Commentary explains about Job 16:21, based on the King James Version of Job 16:21: "O that one might plead for a man with God, as a man pleadeth for his neighbor!"

In Job 16:21: **one**—rather, "He" (referring to God). "Oh, that He would plead for a man (namely, me) against God." Job quaintly says, "God must support me against God; for He makes me to suffer, and He alone knows me to be innocent." God in Jesus Christ does plead with God for man (Rom. 8:26, Rom. 8:27).

as a man—literally in Hebrew, "the Son of man." A prefiguring of the advocacy of Jesus Christ, a boon longed for by Job (Job 9:33), though the spiritual pregnancy of his own words, designed for all ages, was but little understood by him .

for his neighbor—literally in Hebrew, "friend." Job himself (Job 42:8) pleaded as intercessor for his "friends," though "his scorners" (Job 16:20); so Jesus Christ the Son of man (Luk. 23:34) does "for friends" (Joh. 15:13-15). [45]

Are you putting the pieces together? In the midst of Job's suffering which foreshadowed the suffering of Christ, he longed for someone to plead for him on his behalf. And that is exactly why Jesus suffered. He became the Son of man to give His life for us and then be our witness, an intercessor advocating for us.

How does 1 John 2:1-2 describe Jesus?

The author of Hebrews explains Jesus' role before God in the terms of one who is an intercessor for us. Please read this as a summary of all that Christ did and what He does now.

Hebrews 5:7-10 ESV In the days of his flesh, Jesus offered up prayers and supplications, with loud cries and tears, to Him who was able to save Him from death, and He was heard because of His reverence. [8]Although He was a son, He learned obedience through what He suffered. [9]And being made perfect, He became the source of eternal salvation to all who obey Him, [10]being designated by God a high priest after the order of Melchizedek.

Hebrews 7:25-26 Consequently, He is able to save to the uttermost those who draw near to God through Him, since He always lives to make intercession for them. [26]For it was indeed fitting that we should have such a high priest, holy, innocent, unstained, separated from sinners, and exalted above the heavens.

What was the purpose and result of Christ's suffering, in your own words?

The last thing that I would like for you to notice from Job's despairing speech is in his closing comments. He is almost completely hopeless, being resigned that his death is near. He says: "Where then is my hope? Who can see any hope for me? "Job 17:15 [HCSB]

In order to turn around his dreadful despair, Job had to see God in a totally different light. This would not happen until later. [46]

Where is your hope?

Please close this lesson by noting the wonderful truth from Hebrews 6:19-20.

Thank You Lord for Your blessing of ____

____

ᔓBlessed be the Name of the Lord.ᔓ

Lesson 18 ᔓ Job 18 and 19

EXPECTING DEATH

Sometimes as I study and write, I listen to instrumental music. As I'm writing now, Cello Sonata in D Minor is playing in the background. The short Sérénade begins with a slow, low, almost harsh, ominous sound. It then grows in intensity and complexity. Then the Finale *begins with a softer and lighter sound, but includes heightened animation. "This piece uses many types of extended cello technique and is considered technically challenging. It is a staple of the modern cello repertoire and is commonly regarded as one of the finest masterpieces written for the instrument."*[47]

This song is a perfect introduction to Bildad's short, harsh, intense speech (Job 18) and Job's reply (Job 19) that ends with an excited expectation of what he will experience one day. Job 19:25-27 is one of the finest statements of faith in all of Scripture. And Job's words have been preserved through another masterpiece of music: Handel's Messiah.

But before we celebrate Job's faith, we must consider Bildad's comments.

Please pray for the Holy Spirit to give you understanding of God's Word.

Please read Job 18:1-21.

[ESV] **Job 18:1** Then Bildad the Shuhite answered and said: [2]How long will you hunt for words? Consider, and then we will speak. [3]Why are we counted as cattle? Why are we stupid in your sight? [4] You who tear yourself in your anger, shall the earth be forsaken for you, or the rock be removed out of its place? [5]Indeed, the light of the wicked is put out, and the flame of his fire does not shine. [6]The light is dark in his tent, and his lamp above him is put out. [7]His strong steps are shortened, and his own schemes throw him down. [8]For he is cast into a net by his own feet, and he walks on its mesh. [9]A trap seizes him by the heel; a snare lays hold of him. [10]A rope is hidden for him in the ground, a trap for him in the path. [11]Terrors frighten him on every side, and chase him at his heels. [12]His strength is famished, and calamity is ready for his stumbling. [13]It consumes the parts of his skin; the firstborn of death consumes his limbs. [14]He is torn from the tent in which he trusted and is brought to the king of terrors. [15]In his tent dwells that which is none of his; sulfur is scattered over his habitation. [16]His roots dry up beneath, and his branches wither above. [17]His memory perishes from the earth, and he has no name in the street. [18]He is thrust from light into darkness, and driven out of the world. [19]He has no posterity or progeny among his people, and no survivor where he used to live. [20]They of the west are appalled at his day, and horror seizes them of the east. [21]Surely such are the dwellings of the unrighteous, such is the place of him who knows not God.

This speech is about the death of the wicked. And it is true. This is a terrible thing to consider: those who do not know God die with no hope. D.L. Moody said that a "man's heart ought to be very tender" when preaching about the doom of the lost.[48]

The problem we find once again with Bildad is that he is unsympathetic and his understanding, while accurate, is inappropriately applied to Job.

Here are a few notes to help you understand some of the poetical statements above:
Verse 4: ***shall the rock be removed out of its place?*** *Will God change everything just for you, Job?*

Verse 13: ***the firstborn of death consumes his limbs.*** *A deadly disease destroys his body.*

Verse 14: ***the king of terrors.*** *Death is personified as a king.*

Please draw a line between verses as I've done above to separate the following passages and then summarize Bildad's comments.

Bildad's attitude: Job 18:1-4

The death of the wicked: Job 18:5-6

The death of the wicked: Job 18:7-10

The death of the wicked: Job 18:11-13

The death of the wicked: Job 18:14-16

The legacy of the wicked: Job 18:17-19

The warning: Job 18:20-21

There is nothing good about Bildad's speech. Even though it is brief, it describes the most horrendous thing that can happen to a person who does not know God. The death of an unbelieving man or woman is horrifying and is the beginning of an eternity of horrific pain and misery.

What is your reaction to the truth about the death of the wicked?

We are going to leave Bildad's speech – standing solemnly as a tombstone over the grave of an unrighteous man. In contrast to that man, we will see the blameless man Job and his description of what he expects in his own death, which he feels is looming on the horizon.

Please read Job 19:1-29.

Job and his friends are infuriated with each other. Job has had enough of his friends' attacks on his integrity, and his friends are adamant in their assessment of his sin. Bildad began both of his speeches (Job 8:2, 18:2) saying "how long" will you talk like this? So Job answers him with his own "how long will you try to crush me with your words?" Job 19:2 [NLT]

Job says, "These ten times you have reproached me" as he refers to the accusations that have been hurled at him and humiliated him over and over and over again.

"Even if I have sinned," Job said in 19:4, "it's *my* sin and not yours. God and I can work things out, so leave me alone." The word Job used ("erred") means "an unintentional sin." Job still defended his integrity and claimed that he had committed no sins worthy of all the suffering he had endured. [49]

What does Job say in the first half of Job 19:5 that indicates the true motive of his friends?

Superiority. Self-preservation. Pride. These self-centered attitudes are so often the real reason for our beliefs and behaviors. We want to be right. We don't want to be wrong. We don't want to change our lifestyle or our outlook. This was the basis for the unwavering stance of Job's three friends. We've touched on this concept before, but it's worth considering again.

In discussions and/or disagreements, do you tend to humiliate others or humble yourself? What have you been learning from our study in the book of Job that you can apply in challenging situations with others?

What is Job's perspective on his situation, according to Job 19:6-20? (Make sure you consider verse 10.)

The disasters and deaths and disease were intended by Satan to make Job curse God. But he didn't. Then Job's wife said—just do it. Curse God and die. But he didn't. Then his friends accused him of secret sins and a hypocritical life and expected his deserved dreadful death. In defense of himself, Job declared that since there was not a problem with his integrity, there had to be a problem with God. He had jumped to the wrong conclusion but he had not cursed God.

Did God wrong Job? Did God treat Job with injustice? Did God consider Job His enemy? Explain your answer.

This chapter contains the most despairing of all of Job's words, even more so than when he cursed the day he was born. Job's agony was at its peak.

What did Job want from his friends, and why, according to Job 19:21-22?

What did Job want to remain, even after he was dead, according to Job 19:23-24?

The last words of criminals about to be executed often represent how they wish to be remembered. Job was no criminal, but expected that his death was imminent and wanted to be remembered as "not guilty."

I can imagine that the next words he utters could be engraved in one of the foundation stones of the eternal heavenly Jerusalem. At the height of his agony and despair, he made a resolute statement of faith, hope and love.

Write Job's words from Job 19:25-27 in this book with your pen of ink!

Hallelujah! Job's words from verses 25-26 are the words that George Frideric Handel recorded immediately following the Hallelujah chorus in his incredible work: Messiah. Job's words begin Part Three: A Hymn of Thanksgiving for the Final Overthrow of Death. Job's words were a wonderful choice to begin the musical celebration of the resurrection of Christ, don't you think?

Please look up the definition of the following word:
Redeemer: Strong's #1350
Hebrew word:
Hebrew definition:

The faith and hope of Job in chapter 19 is the same as that stated in Job 16:19-21: "Even now, behold, my witness is in heaven, and he who testifies for me is on high . . . my eye pours out tears to God, that He would argue the case of a man with God, as a son of man does with his neighbor."

Job's witness, the one who would testify for him, is his kinsmen-redeemer, who shows up to stand on his behalf and pay whatever price is necessary for his rescue, when all of his friends and even his closest family members are against him or afraid of him.

How do the following verses describe Jesus as our Redeemer?
1 Corinthians 6:19-20

1 Peter 1:18-19

Revelation 5:9

Did Job know what or whom he was talking about? He certainly knew that he was referring to God Himself as his Redeemer, and his faith was in Him. But did Job know that Jesus, called Emmanuel—God with us—would be his Redeemer? No. Could this statement refer to Jesus if that was not Job's intention? Yes! 1 Peter 1:10-12 tells us that even the prophets who prophesied of Christ did not understand the full meaning of what they said.

What was prophesied in Isaiah 59:20?

What were the followers of Jesus hoping for and what were they surprised about, according to Luke 24:19-23?

What does Acts 1:3 tell us that Jesus did?

Based on Job's declaration in Job 19:25 and the eye-witness accounts in Luke and Acts, what can you know and rejoice in today?

Now let's consider the mystery of Job's statement. About 2000 years after Job, Jesus lived, died, and lived again. How could Job say, during his lifetime, that his Redeemer was alive?

What did Jesus say about Abraham (who also lived around 2000 years before Christ) and what did He say about Himself, in John 8:56-58?

Not only did Job have unwavering faith that his Redeemer lives, but he also had great hope and anticipation that he would see Him. Job's greatest desire, his all-consuming passion, was to see God with his own eyes.

There's a song about dreaming of heaven and being shown all of its beauty—seeing loved ones and talking with the saints of the ages. But the dreamer keeps saying—I want to see Jesus, for He's the One who died for all!

What is your all-consuming passion? What do you think about and long for more than anything else? What do your bank account and daily schedule and Google search history and Facebook posts show to be most important to you?

I am so thankful for the amazing faith of Job. I am so thankful that his inspired words ***were*** *written and will last forever. I am so thankful for his statement, which was possibly the very first declaration about salvation through God in Christ. It's been true since before the foundation of the world. Our Redeemer lives! And because He lives, we can face today and tomorrow and eternity.*

Thank You Lord for Your blessing of ____

____

Blessed be the Name of the Lord.

Lesson 19 ~ Job 20

ZOPHAR ATTACKS!

I want you to know that there are times when I read a passage of Scripture and I wonder: "why is ***this*** *in the Bible?" Why do I need to know this? That is how I feel when I read Zophar's speech in Job 20.*

But I know that ***all*** *Scripture is inspired by God (2 Timothy 3:16) and has been recorded and preserved for His good purposes, so I read on. We must hear what Zophar has to say about the ways of the wicked and the future that will come to those who remain in rebellion to the Lord.*

This chapter is definitely profitable for rebuking, correcting, and training us to flee from sin and to seek the righteousness of the Lord. This chapter is also a powerful reminder to us of the terrible, heart-breaking, eternal consequences that will come to those who do not trust in Christ.

Eliphaz described the fate of a wicked man (Job 15) in his attempt to make Job repent, and his description focused on the destruction of the wicked man's (i.e., Job's) property and prosperity. Bildad's speech about the death of the wicked (Job 18) described some of the physical suffering that an unrepentant man (i.e. Job) experiences at his death. Now Zophar describes the death of the wicked – in terms of how the sin of the wicked (i.e. Job) poisons his very being and brings about his own destruction.

~ Please pray for understanding of the Scriptures inspired by the Holy Spirit. ~

Please read Job 20:1-29.

Why does Zophar speak up this time, according to Job 20:1-3?

Zophar needed training in communication. What does the Lord teach us in the following verses?

Lesson #1: Proverbs 15:1

Lesson #2: Proverbs 15:18

Lesson #3: Proverbs 17:27

Lesson #4: Ecclesiastes 7:9

Lesson #5: James 1:19-20

Zophar speaks sharply to Job because he feels insulted. He speaks to defend himself. It is more important to Zophar that he is right than it is for Job to be counseled. In his anger, he lashes out at Job and expounds upon the judgment that will come upon the wicked. Zophar means that this judgment is coming upon Job. And he doesn't care. He gives Job no hope.

In the first phase of his attack, Zophar says the wicked don't live long. What are some of his statements that indicate this, according to Job 20:4-11?

Warren Wiersbe, in his commentary on Job: Be Patient, says:

> Most of the people in Scripture who pondered the problem of evil in the world started from a different premise—the wicked enjoy long life and freedom from trouble, while the righteous suffer much and die young (Psalm 37; 73; Jeremiah 12:1-4). Zophar was deliberately blocking out a lot of data to prove his point. It's amazing how some godless people live to an old age. Perhaps this is the grace of God in giving them time to repent. [50]

Do you ever find yourself desiring the death of the wicked? Is there anyone for whom you can pray that God will give them life and salvation rather than an early death?

In the second phase of his attack, Zophar says that the pleasure of wickedness is temporary and results in punishment.

According to Job 20:12-19, what phrases indicate:

Enjoyment of Evil	End-results of Evil

Perhaps you are wondering about the statement in Job 20:16: "he will suck the poison of the cobras; the viper's tongue will slay him." <u>The Shepherd's Notes Commentary</u> *says: "It may be that Zophar is saying that the wicked participate in their own demise by voluntarily giving themselves to the serpent. The tongue of the snake naturally recalls the speaking snake, the embodiment of evil, in Genesis 3."* [51]

What does James 1:13-15 teach us and how does it relate to the comment from *The Shepherd's Notes*?

Rather than attacking someone who is caught up in the enjoyment of their sin, how and why would you advise them to turn away from it? Differing situations may impact your answer.

In the third phase of his attack, Zophar says that God's judgment will be agonizing.

What words or phrases in Job 20:20-29 express the wrath of God against an unrepentant wicked man?

Zophar's attitude about and application of the fate of the wicked are wrong. But his statements about their destiny are accurate. The rest of Scripture validates his words. God will judge the wicked, and they will experience eternal torment.

Note what the following verses tell you about the judgment of God and the destiny of the wicked.

Genesis 18:25

Psalm 11:6

Isaiah 3:11

Matthew 13:41-42, 49-50

Matthew 25:30

Revelation 20:11-15

Zophar was so intent on being right that he said Job was going to hell. I would rather be wrong about the existence of hell than right about it, but God's word tells us that it is a real place.

What would you say to someone to warn him or her about hell? And the more important question is: How would you warn them? With what attitude and emotion would you tell someone about the reality of hell?

May Zophar's harsh words sound an alarm that causes us to remember the reality of hell and be ready to offer the hope of heaven.

How can a wicked man or woman have hope for heaven according to the following verses?
Ezekiel 18:30-32

Ezekiel 36:26-27

Acts 2:38

Titus 3:4-7

What does 1 Peter 3:15 tell us?

How would you share this hope for heaven in your own words?

This has been a difficult chapter to study. In my opinion, it is one of the most distressing chapters in the whole Bible because it states the fate of the wicked and offers no hope for them. But it has challenged me to be grieved over the destiny of the wicked. It has challenged me to be careful in my attitude of sharing what I believe about hell. It has challenged me to be ready to share the great hope that we have in the grace of God and our Savior Jesus and the life-giving Holy Spirit.

This hope does not disappoint, because God's love has been poured out in our hearts through the Holy Spirit who was given to us. Romans 5:5 HCSB

Thank You Lord for Your blessing of ______________________________

____

∾Blessed be the Name of the Lord.∾

Lesson 20 ~ Job 21

THEY LIVE LONG AND PROSPER

If you are a Star Trek fan, you certainly recognize Dr. Spock's greeting "Live long and prosper," which accompanied his Vulcan salute. But did you know that it is an abbreviated version of a common Jewish blessing? "Shalom aleichem" means "peace be upon you." This shalom is a complete peace, a state of health and well-being, a prosperity in life, in body and soul. "Live long and prosper" is actually a pretty good paraphrase of the blessing!

We learned early on in our study that Job wasn't Jewish, and of course he wasn't Vulcan either! He doesn't state this greeting but he points out that despite Zophar's adamant announcement that the wicked die young, some of them do live long and prosperous lives.

Together, Job 20 and Job 21 present one of the paradoxes of life. This is true: God judges the wicked (Job 20). And this is true too: The wicked live long and prosper (Job 21).

~ Please pray for the Holy Spirit to give you understanding of God's Word. ~

Please read Job 21:1-34.

In Job 21:1-5, what did Job tell his friends to do, that they had obviously not been doing?

Job acknowledges in verse 4 that his complaint is not against man; and by saying this, he implies that his complaint is against God. In verse 6, he indicates that what he is going to say terrifies him. He is astounded because the points he will make prove that God allows circumstances in life that make no sense to our finite minds, especially when we are aware of His holiness and justice.

Write out Job's perplexing question from Job 21:7.

What evidence does Job give of the prosperity of the wicked, in Job 21:8-13? (By the way, in verse 9, the original Hebrew says their houses have "shalom.")

What do the wicked say to God, according to Job 21:14-15?

Have you ever heard anyone say something like that? What was/or is their life like?

It's all very confusing, isn't it? Job 21:16 is also confusing. "Behold, their prosperity is not in their hand; the counsel of the wicked is far from me." NAS Remember, when you see the word "behold," there is something surprising about to be said. The NLT is the easiest to understand: "They think their prosperity is of their own doing, but I will have nothing to do with that kind of thinking." Job shows his wisdom here, acknowledging that God is sovereign even over the prosperity of the wicked.

In verses 17 and 18, Job replies to both Bildad and Zophar. Bildad had said that the lamp of the wicked was quickly snuffed out (Job 18:5, 12) and Zophar had said that the wicked died early in life (Job 20:8-9). Job responds to their declarations with "how often" does that really happen?

Job is probably quoting an ancient saying in verse 19: "God stores up a man's punishment for his sons." What does Job want God to do instead, according to Job 21:19-21?

The wisdom of Job and the solution to all paradoxes is found in Job 21:22. What must we always remember?

Who are the ones "on high" that will be judged? I find it very interesting that the same Hebrew word "rum", which means "to be high, lofty, raised up," is used in Isaiah 14:13 to describe Satan: "You said in your heart, 'I will ascend to heaven; above the stars of God I will set my throne on high; I will sit on the mount of assembly in the far reaches of the north.'" ESV It is also used in Daniel 11:36 to describe the Antichrist: "And the king shall do as he wills. He shall exalt himself and magnify himself above every god, and shall speak astonishing things against the God of gods." ESV

Even though Job did not know that Satan had challenged the Lord's worthiness of worship, he indicated in Job 21:22 that angels would be judged. Eliphaz had already mentioned this in Job 4:18.

How did Job exalt the Lord and bless Him instead of curse Him in his statements about the prosperity of the wicked?

What is the point that Job is making in his comparison of two men, in Job 21:23-26?

How does Job challenge his friend's perspective, according to Job 21:27-29?

The confusing paradoxes keep coming. Job makes a statement in verse 30 that has been translated with two opposite interpretations.

What does your version of Job 21:30 say? The HCSB, ESV, NIV, and NLT present one interpretation. The KJV, NAS, and NKJV present the opposite interpretation. Please note both translations.

Given the context of Job's speech, which version of Job 21:30 do you think is appropriate?

Job, who lived after the flood (Job 38:25-28), and therefore after Enoch (Genesis 5:18-32), may well have known of Enoch's prophecy regarding the eternal future of the wicked.

What did Enoch prophesy, according to Jude 1:14-15?

Job is talking about the experience of the wicked on the earth—where the wicked do prosper and even avoid catastrophes in their lives. He and his friends were dealing with Job's current situation, which they continued to explain was due to his sin. Job presents the prosperity of the wicked as evidence that God allows things to happen in our lives that don't make sense to us!

What else does Job say that is surprising about the wicked, in Job 21:31-33?

His friends are about to get the message. They are about to realize they need to be quiet. Job ends his speech saying, "So how can you console me with your nonsense? Nothing is left of your answers but falsehood!" Job 21:34 NIV

Job reckoned their answers as falsehood, meaning their explanations were filled with treacherous ideas which lacked divine enlightenment.[52]

We must have divine enlightenment before we can know and speak about the ways of the Lord. It is only because He has revealed Himself to us that we know anything about Him. Let's accept the paradoxes presented today through the truth presented by the apostle Paul.

How does Romans 11:33-36 console you when you face strange, confusing circumstances?

May we give glory to God and bless His name, whether the wicked live long and prosper or we suffer and grieve. Bless the Lord today, no matter what you are experiencing.

Thank You Lord for Your blessing of ______________________________

____

Blessed be the Name of the Lord.

Lesson 21 ~ Job 22

ELOQUENT CONDEMNATION FROM ELIPHAZ

We've arrived at the third round of speeches between Job and his friends. Everyone is upset, tempers are flaring, and each man is set in his own interpretation of Job's circumstances. No one believes that Job is blameless, upright, fearing God and shunning evil. Their dialogues have been a little bit like the following routine performed by the Vaudeville comedians Abbott and Costello, without the humor. Abbott, like Job, knows exactly what he's talking about, and his friend just doesn't understand.

Costello: Look Abbott, if you're the coach, you must know all the players.

Abbott: I certainly do.

Costello: Well you know I've never met the guys. So you'll have to tell me their names, and then I'll know who's playing on the team.

Abbott: Well, let's see, we have on the bags, Who's on first, What's on second, I Don't Know is on third...

Costello: That's what I want to find out.

Abbott: I say Who's on first, What's on second, I Don't Know's on third.

Costello: You gonna be the coach?

Abbott: Yes.

Costello: And you don't know the fellows' names?

Abbott: Well I should.

Costello: Well then who's on first?

Abbott: Yes.

Costello: I mean the fellow's name.

Abbott: Who.

Costello: The guy on first.

Abbott: Who.

Costello: The first baseman.

Abbott: Who.

Costello: The guy playing...

Abbott: Who is on first!

Costello: I'm asking YOU who's on first.

Abbott: That's the man's name.[53]

I hope you enjoyed a smile for a moment! There hasn't been anything funny in the story of Job. And now, get ready for the last big speech from one of the three threatening friends. Eliphaz has a lot to say and thinks he knows exactly **who** *is to blame for Job's suffering.*

ᔓ Please pray for the Holy Spirit to give you understanding of God's Word. ᔓ

Please read Job 22:1-30. *I've created paragraphs in Eliphaz's speech to help you see the different sections of his comments. Label the topic of each section in the margin.*

Job 22:1-30 ESV Then Eliphaz the Temanite answered and said: [2]"Can a man be profitable to God? Surely he who is wise is profitable to himself. [3]Is it any pleasure to the Almighty if you are in the right, or is it gain to him if you make your ways blameless? [4]Is it for your fear of him that he reproves you and enters into judgment with you?

[5]Is not your evil abundant? There is no end to your iniquities. [6]For you have exacted pledges of your brothers for nothing and stripped the naked of their clothing. [7]You have given no water to the weary to drink, and you have withheld bread from the hungry. [8]The man with power possessed the land, and the favored man lived in it. [9]You have sent widows away empty, and the arms of the fatherless were crushed. [10]Therefore snares are all around you, and sudden terror overwhelms you, [11]or darkness, so that you cannot see, and a flood of water covers you.

[12]Is not God high in the heavens? See the highest stars, how lofty they are!

[13]But you say, "What does God know? Can he judge through the deep darkness? [14]Thick clouds veil him, so that he does not see, and he walks on the vault of heaven."

[15]Will you keep to the old way that wicked men have trod? [16]They were snatched away before their time; their foundation was washed away. [17]They said to God, "Depart from us," and "What can the Almighty do to us?" [18]Yet He filled their houses with good things - but the counsel of the wicked is far from me. [19]The righteous see it and are glad; the innocent one mocks at them, [20] saying, "Surely our adversaries are cut off, and what they left the fire has consumed."

[21]Agree with God, and be at peace; thereby good will come to you. [22]Receive instruction from his mouth, and lay up his words in your heart. [23]If you return to the Almighty you will be built up; if you remove injustice far from your tents, [24]if you lay gold in the dust, and gold of Ophir among the stones of the torrent bed, [25]then the Almighty will be your gold and your precious silver.

[26]For then you will delight yourself in the Almighty and lift up your face to God. [27]You will make your prayer to him, and he will hear you, and you will pay your vows. [28]You will decide on a matter, and it will be established for you, and light will shine on your ways. [29]For when they are humbled you say, "It is because of pride"; but he saves the lowly. [30]He delivers even the one who is not innocent, who will be delivered through the cleanness of your hands.

What is wrong with Eliphaz's statements in Job 22:1-5? (Consider Job 1:1, 8-12)

The very thing that Job has clung to—his blameless character and fear of God—is now being attacked as worthless. Once again, I can hear the hiss of Satan in the words of Eliphaz, tempting Job to abandon his devotion to the Lord and His righteousness.

What does Ephesians 1:4 tell us about God's plans for us?

And 2 Thessalonians 2:13-15?

And what is the confidence that we have according to Romans 8:1-2?

"To be profitable" in Job 22:2 is based on the verb "sākan," which basically means "to be of use, to be of service." How was Job of service to God?

How is your life of use to God?

Look back at what Eliphaz said in his first speech in Job 4:2-4. What's the difference between his earlier words and Job 22:5-11?

Look at how Job describes his life in Job 29:1-25. Was Eliphaz accurate in his accusation? Explain your answer.

> Not being able to point to specific sins in Job's life, Eliphaz now began to speculate on what Job's sin must have been. [54]

Compare Job 22:12-13 with Job 21:22. Eliphaz was either hard of hearing or a terrible listener. Maybe both! What did Job actually say?

Compare Job 22:15-20 with Job 21:13-17 in the boxes below. Highlight the exact quotes between the two passages, and circle the statements that present opposite views. The underlined statement carries the same meaning in both passages.

Job 21:13-18ESV [13]They spend their days in prosperity, and in peace they go down to Sheol. [14]They say to God, "Depart from us! We do not desire the knowledge of your ways. [15]What is the Almighty, that we should serve him? And what profit do we get if we pray to him?" [16]Behold, is not their prosperity in their hand? The counsel of the wicked is far from me. [17]"How often is it that the lamp of the wicked is put out? That their calamity comes upon them? That God distributes pains in his anger? [18]That they are like straw before the wind, and like chaff that the storm carries away?"	**Job 22:15-20**ESV [15]Will you keep to the old way that wicked men have trod? [16]They were snatched away before their time; their foundation was washed away. [17]They said to God, "Depart from us," and "What can the Almighty do to us?" [18]Yet he filled their houses with good things - but the counsel of the wicked is far from me. [19]The righteous see it and are glad; the innocent one mocks at them, [20]saying, "Surely our adversaries are cut off, and what they left the fire has consumed."

Eliphaz is twisting Job's words and changing his own views as well. Job's friends have been saying that God blesses the righteous and punishes the wicked; but now, Eliphaz declares that God fills the house of the wicked with good things!

Remember, Job's friends were healthy, wealthy, and wise . . . in their own eyes. And they wanted to stay that way. They didn't want to end up like Job, so they had to explain his circumstances in a way that would not jeopardize their own lifestyles. Eliphaz puts an eloquent yet inaccurate spin on Job's words so that they would suit his worldview. He says that Job is a hypocrite who has hidden his sin from everybody but God and now he is receiving what he deserves.

Do you ever twist the facts to suit your own purposes? Do you point out others' faults or accuse them of wrongs so that you will appear to be better than they are?

At the end of Eliphaz's accusation, he offers assistance. But these words carry temptation just as his opening words did.

Let's give Eliphaz the benefit of the doubt and assume that he sincerely wanted to help Job. What actions did he urge Job to take, in Job 22:21-27?

This call for Job to submit; to be at peace with God (v.21); to hear God's word and hide it in his heart (v.22); to return to the Almighty and forsake wickedness (v.23); to find delight in God rather than in gold (vv.24-26); and to pray, obey (v.27), and become concerned about sinners (vv.29-30) could not be improved on by prophet or evangelist. [55]

There are some problems, however, that beset these powerful words. They assume Job was an ungodly man and that his major desire was a return to health and prosperity (v.21). The fact is that Job was not ungodly and that he had already made clear his desire to see God and be his friend (19:25-27).[56]

What are the benefits of Job's repentance, according to Eliphaz, in Job 22:21-30?

Here he [Eliphaz] emphasizes restored favor with God but with the twist that renewed favor will put Job in a position to influence God. This is a more subtle temptation for Job to respond in anticipation of benefits, rather than retain righteousness for the righteousness' sake (as Job has maintained all along). The lure of possessions has now been displaced by the lure for power. "Think of all the good you can do!" [57]

Do you think that your prayers and obedience to God give you "bargaining power" with Him? Is your behavior toward God based more on what **He** wants or what **you** want?

*Remember the comedy routine in the introduction? The question that we need to ask is not "Who's **on** first?," but we need to ask "Who **is** first?"*

This is what the LORD, the King of Israel and its Redeemer, the LORD of Hosts, says:
I am the first and I am the last. There is no God but Me. Isaiah 44:6

Blessed be the Name of the Lord.

Lesson 22 ∾ Job 23 and 24

JOB'S ELOQUENT ANSWER TO ELIPHAZ

Are you weary of arrogant and antagonistic speeches from Job's friends? Are you weary of Job's suffering? How long would you have lasted in the debate if you had been Job? Don't forget that he is absolutely miserable from some kind of skin disease; he can't eat; he can't sleep; and his children have tragically died. His friends keep telling him that it's his own fault.

Charles Swindoll, a pastor and author, calls Job "a man of heroic endurance."[58] *Have you considered Job a hero? Have you considered him as a hero of faith as well as one of patience? It's Job's turn to speak in this third round of the debate. We will see that he is still in deep, dark despair; yet he has faith in God, faith in God's purpose and faith in God's justice.*

∾ Please pray for understanding of the Scriptures inspired by the Holy Spirit. ∾

Please read Job 23:1-24:25.

What verses stand out to you as meaningful or intriguing? Choose two and write them below.

These two chapters are fascinating to me. The first one shows us that Job trusts God to take care of him, and the second one shows us that Job trusts God to "take care of" the wicked. But these two chapters are also perplexing. We are considering the mysterious timing and sovereignty and transcendence of God. And . . . the Hebrew of Job 24 is extremely difficult to translate and interpret; it is often considered the most difficult and most obscure portion of the entire Old Testament. Many scholars think that the speech found in Job 24 should be attributed to Zophar rather than Job. I agree with the comments of Mr. Smick, from The Expositor's Bible Commentary:

> Since there is absolutely no agreement about handling chapter 24, it seems wiser to let the text stand and above all refuse to force modern categories of logic and rhetoric on it. [59]

Let the text stand as it is—yes, let's do that. I promise to do my best to keep things as simple as possible as we study these chapters! Your Bibles will probably have footnotes regarding different translations. Take a look at them just to be aware of them, but try not to get bogged down in the differences. Here we go!

How does Job express his suffering now, according to Job 23:2 and 17?

My sighs bear no proportion to my sufferings. They are no adequate expression of my woes. If you think I complain; if I am heard to groan, yet the sufferings which I endure are far beyond what these would seem to indicate.[60]

In spite of his misery, Job still wants to stand before God in court. What does he expect that experience would hold for him, according to Job 23:3-7?

Based on all that Job has been saying in all of his speeches, we can understand that he expects God to listen to him, to agree with his claim of blamelessness, and to vindicate him. There is, however, a problem in Job's attitude. He wants to correct the Lord. But even in the midst of that wrong thinking, Job is making a statement of trust that God is truly a God of justice.

Have you noticed that the only thing that Job is asking of God is that he be declared "not guilty"? Wow. Let that sink in.

Job doesn't want to ask for his former life back; he doesn't want to ask for his children back; he doesn't want to ask for his sickness to be healed; he doesn't even want to ask for his friends to be slapped in the face by the hand of God! He only wants to be "delivered forever from His Judge."

This is the very thing that every human needs. And deliverance has been provided by our Redeemer—Jesus Christ. Colossians 2:13-14 tells us: "And you, who were dead in your trespasses and the uncircumcision of your flesh, God made alive together with him, having forgiven us all our trespasses, by canceling the record of debt that stood against us with its legal demands. This he set aside, nailing it to the cross."[ESV]

When you stand before God your Judge, what will He declare about you? Guilty or not guilty? Why?

Job wants to stand before God. He can't find Him but he has faith in Him. We might say he feels there is "no God" but he still "knows God."

Please consider the situation he describes in Job 23:8-9 and his walk of faith in Job 23:10-12. How is Job's heroic faith an example for our own lives?

Please look up the definition for the following word:
Tried (Tested): Strong's #974
Hebrew word:
Hebrew definition:

What are some of the ways that the Lord has "tried" you?

What is the outcome of the Lord's testing of us, according to the following verses?
Zechariah 13:9

James 1:2-4

1 Peter 1:7

Please don't miss the reason that Job has the walk of faith that he has. What is the priority of Job's life, according to Job 23:11-12? Is there evidence of this priority in your life?

Somehow, by divine revelation through the Spirit of God, Job knew the words and ways of God. And he also knew the attributes of God.

What are the mysterious qualities of God declared in Job 23:13-14?

How does Job respond to them, in Job 23:15-16?

God doesn't ask our permission. He doesn't tell us His plan ahead of time. He doesn't give us a preview of coming attractions and then add, "Is that okay with you?" And He doesn't explain why it's so hard. He doesn't let you know how it's going to end. He doesn't tell you how long this particular episode is going to last. [61]

I have gulped in shock and awe at times when I have considered these truths about the Lord. I have been afraid at times at what He might allow to happen to me or to those close to me. I realize however that I sometimes fear pain, grief, and suffering more than I fear the Lord Himself. Job's reaction was more appropriate. He actually feared God, with the strongest emotional and reverential fear possible.

Everything that Job has said has been said out of the midst of his great physical misery, emotional grief, and spiritual despair. He called it a darkness and deep gloom. Job's faith in the midst of this darkness was a sacrifice of praise.

Job's faith in God and in His mysterious ways is also expressed in Job 24:1-25. Here's a list of the wickedness that Job is aware of in the world:

- *Stealing of land and livestock (Job 24:2)*
- *Abuse of widows and orphans (Job 24:3)*
- *Stripping the clothing from the poor, exposing them to the elements (Job 24:4-9)*
- *Mistreating employees (Job 24:10-11)*
- *Murder, adultery, theft (Job 24:13-17)*

With all this in mind, what is Job's **question** in verse 1, his **concern** in verse 12, and his **conclusion** in verses 23-24?

There is clearly a delay in God's judgment on the wicked. What would happen if God struck down every wicked person at the moment of his evil act? Would you want Him to do this?

The Lord spoke to Israel through the prophet Isaiah, explaining that He was delaying His anger against them. What was His purpose, according to Isaiah 48:9-11?

And what should we know about the timing of the Lord, according to 2 Peter 3:8-10?

Surely Job would have been concerned about the justice of God being carried out on the wicked who had attacked, burned, and stolen his property. His patience and faith were being stretched to the limits in every way possible. How much more could he take?

A sweet (and funny) friend of mine shared with me that she was going through a long period of hard times. And she said, "I'm expecting too much from my coffee! But I can and should expect an abundance of strength and grace from the Lord." [62]

Please read 2 Corinthians 12:7-10 and write out a prayer based on the promise given here.

ᔓBlessed be the Name of the Lord.ᔓ

Lesson 23 ~ Job 25 and 26

BILDAD TRIES TO BE WISE

Do you have a nickname? Do you have a nickname for someone you know? I have wanted to give Job's friends nicknames throughout this entire study. Their names just don't roll off my tongue. Elī, Bil, and Zo would have been my versions for Eliphaz, Bildad and Zophar. I often think of Bildad as "little Bil" because his speeches were the shortest of the three friends.

We have come to "little Bil's" shortest speech of all. It's only six verses long (Job 25:1-6)! And he is the last of Job's friends to speak in their three-round debate. There's a book named "Your God is Too Small" and that title could be given to Bildad's speech. Bildad shows his own little mind, even as he accurately describes the greatness of God. At first it sounds great. But when we understand his point and see how Job responds to him (Job 26:1-14), we'll see that Bildad was going for one final knockout punch to make Job crumble in desperate false repentance. Stay tuned for Job's resolute declaration of his integrity in Job 27:1-6.

~ Please pray for understanding of the Scriptures inspired by the Holy Spirit. ~

Please read Job 25:1-6 and Job 26:1-4.

What are the great things about God stated in Job 25:1-3? (Try to make 5 statements.)

Bildad isn't saying anything to Job that Job hasn't already declared:

Job 9:4[NKJ]	God is wise in heart and mighty in strength. Who has hardened himself against Him and prospered?
Job 16:19[NKJ]	Surely even now my witness is in heaven, And my evidence is on high.
Job 13:11[NET]	Would not His splendor terrify you and the fear He inspires fall on you?
Job 23:15[NKJ]	Therefore I am terrified at His presence; when I consider this, I am afraid of Him.
Job 19:12[NKJ]	His troops come together and build up their road against me; they encamp all around my tent.
Job 12:22[NET]	He reveals the deep things of darkness, and brings deep shadows into the light.

What does Bildad say (Job 25:4-6) that has already been said before by Eliphaz (Job 4:15-19, Job 15:14-16), and who said it to Eliphaz?

Please turn back to Lesson 8, pages 40-41 to refresh your memory on the problem with the source of the question posed by Eliphaz and Bildad. Briefly note what you learned.

Now let's look at what Job has said—asking questions and using terms appropriately:

Job 9:2NKJ How can a man be righteous before God?
Job 14:4NKJ Who can bring a clean thing out of an unclean? No one!
Job 22:12NKJ Is not God in the height of heaven? And see the highest stars, how lofty they are!
Job 7:17 HCSB What is man, that You think so highly of him and pay so much attention to him?
Job 7:5HCSB My flesh is clothed with maggots and encrusted with dirt, my skin forms scabs and then oozes.
Job 17:13-15ESV If I hope for Sheol as my house, if I make my bed in darkness, if I say to the pit, "You are my father," and to the worm, "my mother," or "my sister," where then is my hope? Who will see my hope?

Is man nothing more than a creation of matter, a creature destined to destruction? No!

What gives significance to man? Answer this according to Genesis 1:27 and Psalm 139:13-16.

If this is the source of our significance, then what is critical for us to believe in order to have the right view of ourselves?

Humans are God's special creation, corrupted by iniquity but bearing God's image nevertheless. Job was not worthless, as Bildad charged. He was of great value to his Maker.[63]

Bildad wanted to trap Job in his depravity. Bildad declared God to be infinite and man (Job) to be finite, with a futile existence, giving him no hope for the future. He wanted Job to know that he had a very limited relationship with God. Little Bil actually had a little God. Job will exert great effort to declare the greatness of God as well as God's incredible, interactive relationship with man. Job will soon quote the words of God spoken to man (Job 28:28).

Which is a greater view of God: that He made man who corrupted himself and He leaves him that way, or that He made man who corrupted himself and provides deliverance for him?

It is disturbing to see how Job's friends speak so knowingly about God when, in the end, God revealed that they really didn't know what they were talking about. Too often, those who say the most about God know the least about God.[64]

Job is disturbed alright! No sweet little nicknames for little Bil. Job speaks directly to him – his speech uses the second person singular pronoun "you," instead of the plural pronoun (you, all of you, y'all, youse guys, you'uns) that he has been using when responding to his friends. He will speak to them collectively again, but right now . . .it's to Bildad . . . You . . .! You . . .! You ! And Job slams Bildad with sarcasm.

What are some of Job's strong, sharp remarks to Bildad, in Job 26:2-4?

Ok. Enough already. No use wasting words on Bildad's babble. It's no use belittling little Bil any longer. Job quickly begins to recount God's greatness with a hymn to the cosmic power of God.[65] *The version below is closest to the original Hebrew. There are explanatory notes on the next page. I've placed Bildad's words next to it so that we can see why Job quoted this poem.*

Please read Job 26:5-13, then complete the exercise below the passage.

Job 26:5-13[NAS]

Job's Hymn to the Cosmic Power of God

[5]The departed spirits tremble under the waters and their inhabitants. [6]Naked is Sheol before Him and Abaddon has no covering. [7]He stretches out the north over empty space, and hangs the earth on nothing. [8]He wraps up the waters in His clouds; and the cloud does not burst under them. [9]He obscures the face of the full moon, and spreads His cloud over it. [10]He has inscribed a circle on the surface of the waters, at the boundary of light and darkness. [11]The pillars of heaven tremble, and are amazed at His rebuke. [12]He quieted the sea with His power, and by His understanding He shattered Rahab. [13]By His breath the heavens are cleared; His hand has pierced the fleeing serpent.

Job 25:1-6[NAS]

Bildad's Echo of Eliphaz's Night Vision

Then Bildad the Shuhite answered, [2]"Dominion and awe belong to Him Who establishes peace in His heights. [3]Is there any number to His troops? And upon whom does His light not rise? [4]How then can a man be just with God? Or how can he be clean who is born of woman? [5]If even the moon has no brightness And the stars are not pure in His sight, [6]how much less man, that maggot, and the son of man, that worm!" **Job 26:1** Then Job responded, [2]"What a help you are to the weak! How you have saved the arm without strength! [3]What counsel you have given to one without wisdom! What helpful insight you have abundantly provided! [4]To whom have you uttered words? And whose spirit was expressed through you?"

Highlight the similar or contrasting topics between the two passages. Look for concepts such as: the spirit world, high and low places, the universe, light and dark, awe/reverence, God's power.

Here are some explanatory notes:
Job 26:5 – Departed spirits: the Hebrew "*Rephaim*" designates "shades" or "spirits" and refers to the inhabitants of the netherworld.
Job 26:6 – Sheol and Abaddon: used here as parallel terms for the grave, the place of the dead, and the place of destruction.
Job 26:8 – Clouds: The fact that God can spread out the heavens over empty space, hang the earth on nothing, and fill the clouds with water without their bursting is intended to make us stand in awe (v.8). Those clouds, though they contain an impressive quantity of water, do not split and dump all the water at once. Even with today's scientific explanation of cloud formation in terms of temperature, pressure, condensation, etc., one is still moved to wonder at the extreme complexity and yet ingenious simplicity of such a phenomenon.[66]
Job 26:10 – A circle on the face of the waters: this may refer to the horizon, seen as a circle because of the earth's circular, globe-shaped sphere.[67] It also seems to refer to God's act at creation of separating the light from the darkness (Genesis 1:4).
Job 26:11 – The pillars of heaven: a poetic phrase for the mountains; they rest on the earth, but they seem to hold up the heavens.[67]
Job 26: 12 – Rahab: as mentioned previously, the Hebrew noun "*rahab*" means pride, arrogance; in this verse and a few other Scriptures it refers to a sea monster, perhaps the same one as Leviathan in Job 3:8, Job 7:12 and Job 9:13. It may be parallel with "the fleeing serpent" in the next verse, as it is in **Isaiah 27:1**[NAS] "In that day the LORD will punish Leviathan the fleeing serpent, with His fierce and great and mighty sword, even Leviathan the twisted serpent; And He will kill the dragon who lives in the sea." It can also mean boisterous behavior and some translate it as "storm."
The heavens are cleared: The Hebrew word for cleared is "*shiphra*." It means to be pleasing, beautiful and fair.

When I first read Job's hymn, I caught a glimpse of the greatness of God. The more I've studied it, the more I've been in awe of what is described. I'm bewildered, actually, in trying to understand it all. How could I think that I could understand the mysterious power of my incomprehensible God?

Please re-read Job 26:5-13, then write out Job's humble statement of reverence from Job 26:14.

Who is more worthy of our devotion and obedience: a God we can understand or a God we cannot understand?

The creation of the heavens and the earth is only a hint of what our omnipotent Lord God can do! Seeing all this great creation is like hearing just a whisper from God.

> But with much more impressiveness it may be asked, as Job probably meant to ask, who could understand the great God, if He spoke out with the full voice of His thunder, instead of speaking in a gentle whisper?[69]

There would be a time beyond Job's life when God would speak and people would only hear thunder, not understanding His words. What did God say to Jesus and what would God do by His great power, according to John 12:27-33?

What has been the greatest display of God's power in your life?

I'd like to quote from Charles Swindoll again, from his book about Job.

The study of Job is essentially the study of God Himself. Think about it.

- It was God who first met with Satan and struck the deal regarding Job.
- It was God who released the Adversary to go after Job. It was God who set the boundaries, placing limitations on each attack.
- It was God who permitted all of it to happen, start to finish.
- It was God who broke the silence and spoke to Job.
- And it was God who finally set the record straight, rebuking the "sorry counselors" and rewarding His faithful servant.

All the way through the story, it is God who captures our attention and makes us wonder. Better stated, He confuses us.[70]

Are you content to be confused by God? I hope so, because I've been confused by the 8 verses of this hymn; and when God opens His mouth and speaks to Job, we'll be studying about 100 verses regarding His power!

I began our lesson nicknaming Bildad "little Bil." Through his words and Job's words, I've realized that I'm a little one myself. Jesus loves me this I know, for the Bible tells me so. Little ones to Him belong, they are weak, but He is strong.

Thank You Lord for Your blessing of ____

____

Blessed be the Name of the Lord.

Lesson 24 ∾ Job 27

JOB'S RESOLUTION OF RIGHTEOUSNESS

From the grandeur of God to the groaning of Job . . . The last speech of Job hits highs and lows and depths and desperate declarations. We are about to see how the many disasters in Job's life and the many words of his friends bring him to the point of "justifying himself rather than justifying God." Job 32:2

I'd like for you to have a brief survey of Job's last and longest speech. He has so much to say and the topics change from chapter to chapter. Remember, this is all still written as poetry! It is an incredible work of literature as well as being such an important lesson regarding suffering, wisdom, and the sovereignty of God.

∾ Please pray for the Holy Spirit to give you understanding of God's Word. ∾

Job's Final Speech: Job 26:1 – 31:40 — Please write the verses below next to the topic.

Part One: Job 26

A. Job 26:1-4 - Answering Bildad: **Job 26:1**

B. Job 26:5-14 - Hymn to the Cosmic Power of God: **Job 26:14**

Part Two: Job 27

A. Job 27:1-6 - His Declaration of Righteousness: **Job 27:1, 6**

B. Job 27:7-23 - The Fate of the Wicked: **Job 27:13**

Part Three: Job 28

A. Job 28:1-28 - Where to Find Wisdom: **Job 28:12, 23**

Part Four: Job 29, 30, 31

A. Job 29:1-25 - Job's Past: **Job 29:1-2**

B. Job 30:1-31 - Job's Present: **Job 30:1**

C. Job 31:1-34 - Job's Protest of Innocence: **Job 31:5-6**

D. Job 31:34-40 - Job's Challenge to the Lord: **Job 31:35**

E. The Conclusion: **Job 31:40 (last sentence)**

Now you have an idea of what we will be studying in the next few lessons. Job is right to magnify the power of God. He is right to express that he is not suffering because of obvious sin or hidden sin. But he goes too far in defending himself.

Please note Job's problem as explained by the narrator in Job 32:1-2. It's important for us to keep this in mind as we study Job's speech.

We will consider that statement again after we've read Job 27-31. It's time to see what is considered to be the climax of the "Speak-off." Everything has been leading up to this. Job tells it like it is in his own eyes. I can imagine him even standing up—in all his pain—stomping his foot on the ground, and raising his fisted hand in the air—to declare his perspective and his resolution.

Please read Job 27:1-7.

This is a powerful statement in many ways. We need to remember a few basic facts as we process what Job says.

1. *Job and his three friends believe wholeheartedly that God always acts according to the "retribution principle," so they all believe that the righteous are rewarded and the wicked are punished.*

2. *Job has been described as blameless and upright, fearing God and turning from evil, since Chapter 1.*

3. *Neither Job nor his friends know that Satan incited God against Job. Their understanding is limited concerning Job's suffering and God's actions.*

The first phrase of Job's declaration is hard to handle. He makes an oath based on the existence of God Himself, "As God lives . . ., The Almighty . . . "

How does Job describe God as he makes an oath by His name (Job 27:2)?

"God hasn't been fair to me. God has mistreated me. God has not given me my day in court. God has punished me for crimes I did not commit. He has brought the deepest, darkest pain and grief upon me."

That's Job's perspective. Is it right? (Explain your answer.)

When suffering the bitter trials of life, our vision of God can become obscured, and gross distortions of reality can result. Prolonged pain can lead us to make wrong assumptions about God. When this occurs, all of life gets out of focus.[71]

It's time for a reality check. Do your concepts of God reflect the truth of Who God is as He is revealed in the Bible? That's a hard question to answer if you don't know what the Bible says about God. If what we think about God is the most important thing about us, then knowing and believing and submitting to what the Bible says about God is the most important pursuit of our lives.

What truths about God can you list, with the corresponding scripture references? (The concordance in the back of your Bible might be helpful to you.)

The Scripture reveals that God can always be trusted to do what is right. Listen to the Word, not your worries.[72]

What a comfort it is to know and believe that God will always do what is right. People, even though they mean well, cannot be so trusted. We have regularly observed that Job's friends wrongly accused him of sin. The more they accused him, the more he defended himself and his integrity.

What did Job say to his friends, according to Job 27:3-5(a)?

This is one of Job's ultimate, accurate statements. If he were to give in to his friends urging him to confess sin . . . it would actually be a lie, and that in itself would be a sin!

What was Job's resolute declaration about his integrity, according to Job 27:5(b)-6?

Satan had said, "Does Job fear God for nothing?" (Job 1:9) Here we see that Job is determined to maintain his integrity until the day he dies even though it seems that he will not be rewarded for it. Job's resolution to hold on to blamelessness and uprightness proves Satan wrong. God is to be feared because He is God, not because of what He does or does not do or because of what He gives or takes away.

Are you willing to let your life be evidence before the world and before Satan that God is worthy to be worshipped because of Who He is, even if this means losing everything . . . or giving up your dreams . . . or being ridiculed . . . or experiencing emotional distress… or not getting answers from God?

We've seen good and bad in Job's declaration. He was right and he was wrong at the same time. He had just spoken of the greatness of God (Job 26:5-014), but now he was proclaiming that God had mistreated him. Job was right in proclaiming his integrity, but wrong to find fault with God. He was right all along that God would find him innocent, but wrong that God was punishing him. Job's innocence had slipped into insolence. Pride and self-righteousness had crept in as he had defended himself.

And Job has more to say.

What is Job's desire, according to Job 27:7? To whom is he referring, based on his comments in this verse?

Job's enemies were wrong about him, and in this "prayer" he is asking God to vindicate him by judging them. The rest of the chapter is a description of what comes to the wicked. Once again, the horrible fate of those who are in rebellion to the Lord is described.

Briefly summarize what the wicked will receive from God, according to Job 27:8-23.

No surprises there. The wicked will be judged. But there will be a surprise at the end of the book of Job. God will tell Job to pray for his friends so that they won't be judged as they deserve! (Job 42:7-8)

This has been a really challenging lesson for me . . . because I so often make myself right and others wrong. It's scary to think about having that attitude towards God. What I need is wisdom; discernment; and an accurate assessment of myself, based on an accurate assessment of the Lord. Where can wisdom be found? Job will explain this in the next section of his speech.

Thank You Lord for Your blessing of ____

____

Blessed be the Name of the Lord.

Lesson 25 ~ Job 28

WHERE IS WISDOM?

I have been anticipating the study of this chapter for a while. It is incredibly descriptive and shines with precious truth. Get your ropes, pick axe, and headlamp. We're going mining.

~ Please pray for understanding of the Scriptures inspired by the Holy Spirit. ~

Please read Job 28:1-28.

What precious things does a miner search for, according to Job 28:1-2, and 6?

What does a miner do in his search for precious things, according to Job 28:3-4 and 9-11?

Have you ever been spelunking? Cave exploring? Have you ever been in a cavern deep under a mountain and had the lights turned out? It's the darkest darkness possible! I'm kind of afraid of heights and kind of afraid of depths as well!

My daughter Emily has little fear of either and once led campers in an adventure into a cave in Croatia. She was the only adult small enough to fit into the narrow passages. I'm just glad that I didn't know about her journey under the earth until she had returned safe and sound.

What would you risk your life for? What do you expend incredible effort doing?

What is the focus of Job's poem, according to Job 28:12-21? What should we learn from these verses?

This powerful description of human ability and successful efforts at finding hidden treasures under the surface of the earth contrasts strongly with our inability to find wisdom.[73]

What absolute truth about wisdom is stated in Job 28:23?

Why is that true, according to Job 28:24-27?

I doubt that those concepts surprise you, since you are studying the Bible with me. But let's just think about the world's view on wisdom. Where do people look for it? Age. Experience. Science. Observation of nature. Spirituality. The universe. Every bit of "wisdom" derived from those sources is dependent on a human mind's understanding of what it sees or experiences. That's the problem. The human mind is finite and flawed.

What does James 1:5, 17 say?

What does James 3:13-17 tell us about earthly wisdom versus God's wisdom?

James description of wisdom reflects the truth of God's words to man, quoted in Job 28:28. I am so intrigued by this verse! How did Job know that God said this? Who told him? It isn't quoted anywhere else in the Scriptures. I wonder if the Lord said it to Adam and if this truth was passed down from generation to generation. The Hebrew word used in this verse for "man" is "adam."

What does Job 28:28 say?

Please turn back to Lesson 1, page 15 and note a summary of the definitions of the words "fear" and "turn."

Had Job been living his life according to the wisdom of God? Explain your answer.

Warren Wiersbe gives a complete description of what "fearing the Lord" looks like in our lives. Please read his comments below and on the next page and record the truths from his scripture references.[74] He says:

- It is loving reverence for God, Who He is, what He says, and what He does **(Malachi 2:5-6).**

- It is not a fear that paralyzes, but one that energizes. When you fear the Lord, you obey His commandments **(Eccl. 12:13),**

- walk in His ways **(Deut 8:6),**

- and serve Him **(Josh. 24:14).**

- You are loyal to Him and give Him whole-hearted service **(2 Chronicles 19:9).**

- Like Job, when you fear the Lord, you depart from evil **(Proverbs 3:7-8).**

- The "fear of the Lord" is the fear that conquers fear **(Psalm 112);**

- for if you fear God, you need not fear anyone else **(Matthew 10:26-31).**

Please read Job 28:1-28 once more.

This chapter presents the answer to the question of the whole book of Job and begins to prepare us for God's answer to Job. How are we to understand the mysteries of life? How do we live wisely in the midst of suffering, when nothing makes sense?

What is the wise and right way to live no matter what our circumstances are?

Perhaps you are familiar with a praise song from several years ago. I think it's an appropriate ending for our lesson today. As we pursue wisdom and as we walk in the fear of the Lord, focusing on the Lord Himself is the best thing we can do.

Lord, You are more precious than silver;
Lord, You are more costly than gold;
Lord, You are more beautiful than diamonds;
And nothing I desire compares with You.[75]

Blessed be the Name of the Lord.

Lesson 26 ~ Job 29 and 30

THEN AND NOW

Sometimes it's easier to understand and enjoy a story when you know what to expect. We can understand the Bible better when we look at the big picture as well as the small details. We had a preview of Job's final speech a few lessons ago; now I'd like to give you a summary of Job 29 and 30 before you read them in their entirety. These two chapters depict the reversal of fortunes that Job has experienced.

Job 29: *God was with me! Life was good! The city respected me! I helped those in need! I protected the weak! I expected to live a long life! Men listened to me and I comforted mourners!*

Job 30: *But now. I mourn and sons of fools mock me. I am afflicted. I am weak, and everyone is against me. No one helps me. My pain never ends. God doesn't answer me.*

He is still bewildered as to why this happened to him.

I agree with the Shepherd's Notes Commentary that says: "We should not dismiss chapter 29 as self-pity but should seek for its larger function in the book. That function seems to be to show that Job no longer has any theological missiles to hurl or arguments to build. He is at the end of his rope. He understands nothing of what has happened to him, and he can now only mourn."[76]

Authors of literature throughout history have eloquently expressed the concept that "every memory of a blissful past has a special bitterness of its own. Alfred Lord Tennyson said, 'a sorrow's crown of sorrow is remembering happier things'" [77]

Please pray for understanding of the Scriptures inspired by the Holy Spirit.

Please read Job 29:1 – 30:31.

How does Job begin (Job 29:2) and how does he end (Job 30:31)?

What does Job say about his relationship with God in earlier days, according to Job 29:2-5?

How does Job describe God's interaction with him now, according to Job 30:19-23?

Do you see that Job equated friendship with God with being blessed by Him? Job said that God "watched" (Hebrew: "shamar") over him in the past. "Shamar" is translated as "spare" or "preserve" in Job 2:6. [NET] *So the Lord said to Satan, "All right, he is in your power; only preserve his life."*

Did God stop watching over Job during his suffering? Explain your answer.

Do you think that being in a good relationship with God should always lead to a happy, painless, successful life? If you don't realize it already, please understand that that is the perspective of a prosperity gospel. Please be careful of the mindset "if I trust and obey, I'll get my way."

If we feel that we deserve God's blessing because of our faith and obedience, then when that blessing is disturbed by hardship, we are left confused and angry. Job is a good example of this.... But the Bible, in both Old Testament and New Testament, never promises that God's people will enjoy undisturbed blessings in this life.[78]

Let's look at the good life Job had and the painful life he was enduring, and then we'll come back to the reason for and reality of a relationship with God.

Briefly note some of what Job experienced in his past and in his present in the chart below.

Job 29:5-25 The Good Life	Job 30:1-31 The Bad and Sad Life

We know, based on the first two chapters of Job, that God has watched over Job and has protected him. Even during Satan's attack, God preserved Job's life. And all that God allowed was according to His own divine, sovereign wisdom.

I'd like to remind you of a statement quoted early on in our study. In Lesson 6, I shared:

...when the bad as well as the good is received at the hand of God, every experience of life becomes an occasion of blessing. But the cost is high. It is easier to lower your view of God than to raise your faith to such a height.[79]

I challenged you to join the adventure of having our faith stretched and raised to greater heights than we have known before. Let's look at a few verses that will strengthen our hearts and minds as we continue on this journey, where our hope is not focused on a pain-free life on earth, but where our hope is fixed on the joys of our future with God in our heavenly home.

What was Paul's passion in Philippians 3:10-11?

Where does comfort come from, according to 2 Corinthians 1:3-4?

What is the hope and comfort for those in Christ, according to 1 Thessalonians 4:13-18?

What is the will of the Lord for us, no matter what our circumstances are, according to 1 Thessalonians 5:15-18?

What is an absolute certainty for you to experience if you have placed your faith in Jesus Christ as your Savior, according to Revelation 21:1-5?

That's the good life! This isn't it. When we all get to heaven, what a day of rejoicing it will be!

Please take this opportunity to bless the Lord and thank Him for the good and the bad that He has allowed in your life. He has a purpose for it all.

Thank You Lord for Your blessing of ____

____

Blessed be the Name of the Lord.

Lesson 27 ᔓ Job 31

JOB'S CLOSING ARGUMENT

I am not a legal expert, nor do I enjoy the details of lawsuits and court trials. But of all the aspects of a legal proceeding, the closing argument is the most interesting to me. How does the prosecutor or defense attorney sum up everything that has been presented in the case? What do they highlight as the most important things to take into consideration as the verdict is deliberated?

*Chapter 31 is Job's final statement of innocence. He lists 14 sins that he has not committed; and as he does so, he urges the Lord to bring a proper judgment against him if he has actually committed them. In his last words, rather than cursing God, Job actually calls down curses upon himself—**if** he has sinned. He maintains his integrity and his fear of the Lord against all tragedies, harassments, and confusions.*

Some say that this speech demonstrates a self-righteous attitude; however, it is only the continued and correct declaration of innocence. He rests his case. Job's suffering was never due to sin.

ᔓ Please pray for the Holy Spirit to give you understanding of God's Word. ᔓ

Please read Job 31:1-40.

Using 3 colors, highlight comments about ***God*** in one color, comments beginning with ***if*** in another color, and comments beginning with ***let me*** in another color.

ESV **Job 31:1** I have made a covenant with my eyes; how then could I gaze at a virgin? [2]What would be my portion from God above and my heritage from the Almighty on high? [3]Is not calamity for the unrighteous, and disaster for the workers of iniquity? [4]Does not He see my ways and number all my steps? [5]If I have walked with falsehood and my foot has hastened to deceit; [6] (Let me be weighed in a just balance, and let God know my integrity!) [7]if my step has turned aside from the way and my heart has gone after my eyes, and if any spot has stuck to my hands, [8]then let me sow, and another eat, and let what grows for me be rooted out. [9]If my heart has been enticed toward a woman, and I have lain in wait at my neighbor's door, [10]then let my wife grind for another, and let others bow down on her. [11]For that would be a heinous crime; that would be an iniquity to be punished by the judges; [12]for that would be a fire that consumes as far as Abaddon, and it would burn to the root all my increase. [13]If I have rejected the cause of my manservant or my maidservant, when they brought a complaint against me, [14]what then shall I do when God rises up? When He makes inquiry, what shall I answer Him? [15]Did not He who made me in the womb make him? And did not One fashion us in the womb? [16]If I have withheld anything that the poor desired, or have caused the eyes of the widow to fail, [17]or have eaten my morsel alone, and the fatherless has not eaten of it [18](for from my youth the fatherless grew up with me as with a father, and from my mother's womb I guided the widow), [19]if I have seen anyone perish for lack of clothing, or the needy without covering, [20]if his body has not blessed me, and if he was not warmed with the fleece of my sheep, [21]if I have raised my hand against the fatherless, because I saw my help in the gate, [22]then let my shoulder blade fall from my shoulder, and let my arm be broken from its socket. [23]For I was in terror of calamity from God, and I could not have faced His majesty. [24]If I have made gold my trust or called fine gold my confidence, [25]if I have rejoiced because my wealth was abundant or because my hand had found much, [26] if I have looked at the sun when it shone, or the moon moving in splendor, [27]and my heart has been secretly enticed, and my mouth has kissed my hand, [28] this also would be an iniquity to be punished by the judges, for I would have been false to God above. [29]If I have rejoiced at the ruin of him who hated me, or exulted when evil overtook him [30](I have not let my mouth sin by asking for his life with a curse), [31]if the men of my tent have not said, 'Who is there that has not been filled with his meat?' [32](the sojourner has not lodged in the street; I have opened my doors to the traveler), [33]if I have concealed my transgressions as others do by hiding my iniquity in my bosom, [34]because I stood in great fear of the multitude, and the contempt of families terrified me, so that I kept silence, and did not go out of doors—[35]Oh, that I had one to hear me! (Here is my signature! Let the Almighty answer me!) Oh, that I had the indictment written by my adversary! [36]Surely I would carry it on my shoulder; I would bind it on me as a crown; [37]I would give him an account of all my steps; like a prince I would approach him. [38]If my land has cried out against me and its furrows have wept together, [39]if I have eaten its yield without payment and made its owners breathe their last, [40]let thorns grow instead of wheat, and foul weeds instead of barley. The words of Job are ended.

In this chapter, he cites fourteen types of sin he has not fallen into, a number that is significantly twice seven, a number that signifies completion. The implication of the whole is that his moral character has been wholly flawless, a point that the prologue has already established.[80]

Please circle key words or phrases in the passage above related to the list of sins below. Note the specific sin in the margin next to the verses above.

- Lust (vv. 1-2)
- Being a worker of iniquity (vv. 3-4)
- Lying (vv. 5-6)
- Abandoning good, turning from God (vv. 7-8)
- Adultery (vv. 9-12)
- Cruelty toward slaves (vv. 13-15)
- Apathy towards the poor and suffering (vv.16-23)
- Trust in wealth (vv. 24-25)
- Idolatry and pagan religion (vv. 26-28)
- Spite and hatred (vv. 29-30)
- Being inhospitable to strangers (vv. 31-32)
- Hypocrisy (vv. 33-34)
- Indictment of sin (vv. 35-37)
- Taking land by oppression or extortion (vv. 38-40)

Look back at what you highlighted about God. What does Job know about God and how does he act toward Him?

Job believed that he had lived his life in a way that would withstand God's scrutiny. Job was one who regularly evaluated his life and the lives of his family so that he would continue to walk in the fear of the Lord. This is a good example for us to follow.

Please take inventory of your heart and soul before the Lord. Consider whether you are walking in blamelessness, uprightness, fearing the Lord, and turning from evil in the following categories:

Your thought life
Your business
Your community involvement
Your friendships
Your spiritual gifts
Your family responsibilities
Your vacations
Your promises
Your finances
Your social contacts
Your talents
Your family relationships
Your exercise routine

Please write a prayer for yourself according to 1 Corinthians 10:31.

Based on his innocence, Job makes one final plea. What does he want, according to Job 31:35-37?

Job had repeatedly pleaded for a fair hearing before God (13:18-23, 23:2-7) even though he feared such a meeting (9:14-16) and felt the need for an arbitrator (9:32-35; 16:21). Job nonetheless felt so confident that his integrity would be vindicated that he signed his affidavit. His signature was literally his *tav*, the last letter in the Hebrew alphabet, in the form of an X in ancient Hebrew. The name of the letter means "mark." Documents were usually sealed with an engraved seal (1 Kg 21:8), but when signed by hand even a literate person used the *tav*. When God presented His indictment (7:20), Job would place it proudly on his shoulder and approach the Lord as a prince wearing a victor's crown. Job was certain that he had proven his innocence and righteousness (23:3-7; 27:6). [81]

This is the end of Job as we have known him. His words regarding his innocence are complete. We've seen his best and his worst days so far and have seen a suffering man cling to his faith in his God. But Job thought that God had made a mistake. Job has been longing to appear before God and correct Him. Job definitely had a high view of God but he had come to a higher view of himself and he was the one who needed to be corrected.

Psalm 115:1,3[NIV]
Not to us, O LORD, not to us
but to Your name be the glory,
because of Your love and faithfulness.
Our God is in heaven;
He does whatever pleases Him.

Thank You Lord for Your blessing of ____

____

~Blessed be the Name of the Lord.~

Lesson 28 ~ Job 32 and 33

WHOSE TURN IS IT NOW?

We watch a lot of sports at my house. A lot of sports! Tennis. Football. Football! Football!!! Basketball. Golf. Hockey. Soccer. Baseball. All the Olympics (even curling). And more! One of my favorite commercials over the years is the one where the fans are watching an exciting game at a restaurant and just don't want it to end. So the bartender flips a switch below the counter, causing a surprising play and the game goes into overtime.

Overtime . . . a tiebreaker . . . penalty kicks . . . foul shots . . . the intensity is high, you gear up for one last stand, and the game goes on.

Let me suggest you do that now! This debate is going into overtime. We have a surprising participant joining the discussion. Just when we thought the "Speak-off" had ended with Job's final defense, Elihu opens his mouth. He hasn't been mentioned at all. Maybe that's because no one wanted to him to speak—he is really long-winded! I need not say more, because Elihu will tell you everything he thinks you need to know.

Elihu's speech is the longest of all the speeches in Job, running from Job 32 through Job 37. Based on the repeated phrase: "Elihu . . . said" (Job 32:6; 34:1; 35:1; 36:1), you can see that it's actually 4 speeches in one.

Please pray for understanding of the Scriptures inspired by the Holy Spirit.

What do you learn about Elihu from the following passages? What is his perspective? Feel free to keep your answers short! (Some of his comments are addressed to Job, some are addressed to Eliphaz, Bildad, and Zophar.)

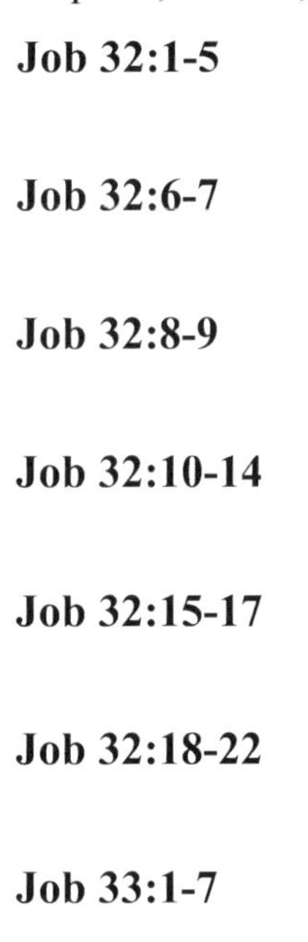

Job 32:1-5

Job 32:6-7

Job 32:8-9

Job 32:10-14

Job 32:15-17

Job 32:18-22

Job 33:1-7

Congratulations! You've heard a chapter's worth of Elihu's introduction! He's been sitting on the bench waiting to get in the game. Now he's all warmed up and ready to make some big plays.

Please look up the meaning of the following names:
Elihu: Strong's #453
Hebrew word:
Hebrew definition:

Barachel: Strong's #1292
Hebrew word:
Hebrew definition:

True to his name, Elihu will defend God's honor, teaching that God mercifully and justly disciplines his servants. His teaching prepares for Yahweh's appearance to Job. [82]

Oh good! There will be accurate statements about God's character and His actions in Elihu's speeches. Keep in mind though that he has said that he is full of words. Many words lead to mistakes: "Indeed, we all make many mistakes. For if we could control our tongues, we would be perfect and could also control ourselves in every other way." James 3:2 [NLT]

Please note his attitude and assessment about Job's situation, based on the following verses:

Job 32:2

Job 33:8-13

Do you see the problem with Job's thinking here? How would you express Elihu's premise in your own words?

Touchdown! Elihu is right! We have to understand this perspective from Elihu to see the value and appropriateness of his speech. He wanted Job to realize that his view about God's justice was wrong. How do we know Elihu is right? Because God will point out the same thing to Job and God does not rebuke Elihu when He rebukes the other friends.

Elihu has a lot to say . . . he's making up for his silence. Eliphaz and Bildad took turns making three speeches, and Zophar made two. Elihu makes four speeches all in a row! He'll express in Speech #1 that God disciplines through suffering to bring a person to repentance. In Speech #2 he explains that God governs the world with justice without exception. In Speech #3 he says that God cannot be bribed or threatened, He remains the same whether men obey or disobey Him. And in Speech #4 he expresses that God is merciful when He disciplines through suffering and that God is sovereign over the unexplainable aspects of nature as well as over unexplainable suffering.

Let's look at Elihu's Speech #1.

Please read Job 33:14-33.

What is the first truth that Elihu wants us to understand, according to Job 33:14?

How does God speak, according to Elihu?

Job 33:15 - through ______________________________

Job 33:19-22 - through ______________________________

Job 33:23 - through ______________________________

Stephen Davey states, "For Job, prior to the completed revelation of God's Word, God could and did speak new truths through dreams and visions. Today, dreams are not intended to communicate **new** revelation from God. They are nothing more than our subconscious minds at work—perhaps working through truths or situations that have impacted us. Dreams can certainly impress us, even when we're asleep. But if they distract us from the revealed truth of God's Word, they are to be discarded as soon as we awaken; if our dreams support the truth of God's Word, then we're really not following a dream, are we? We are remaining committed and surrendered to the revealed Word of God."[83]

The word "chastened" is used in Job 33:19 and means to rebuke, to correct, to convince or convict.

Why does God speak to man in these ways?
Job 33:17

Job 33:24-26

Job 33:28-30

What will be the response of the man disciplined by the Lord, according to Job 33:25-27?

What should our perspective be regarding the discipline of the Lord based on Hebrews 12:5-6?

In *The Problem of Pain,* C.S. Lewis says, "God whispers to us in our pleasures, speaks in our conscience, but shouts in our pains; it is His megaphone to rouse a deaf world." [84]

While we have been intently focusing on the blamelessness of Job and that his suffering was not due to some specific sin in his life, it is true that the Lord may choose to convict us of specific sins through a time of suffering. It is always appropriate to ask the Lord to show us if there is sin to confess. It is the job of the Holy Spirit to convict us and lead us in repentance.

What instruction is given to us in Hebrews 3:7-8?

Please take time to pray that God will make you sensitive to His Holy Spirit's conviction. I want to pay attention to the whispers and words of the Lord before He has to shout at me through pain.

Hebrews 4:12-13 NAS For the word of God is living and active and sharper than any two-edged sword, and piercing as far as the division of soul and spirit, of both joints and marrow, and able to judge the thoughts and intentions of the heart. And there is no creature hidden from His sight, but all things are open and laid bare to the eyes of Him with whom we have to do.

Thank You Lord for Your blessing of ____

____

ᔓBlessed be the Name of the Lord.ᔓ

Well, we've got a lot more of Elihu's words to hear. But let's take a timeout and study the rest of his speeches in the next lesson.

Lesson 29 ᔓ Job 34 and 35

THE BEST DEFENSE

Okay. The timeout is over. Elihu is back in the game and is going to show that the best defense is a good offense. We know that Elihu's "wrath was aroused"—the narrator told us that four times! (Job 32:2-5) And it was because Job "justified himself rather than God." (Job 32:2) Elihu's first move was to point out to Job that "God is greater than man."(Job 33:12) He then expounded on that in his first speech and showed that God allows suffering to discipline his people and bring them to repentance and right relationship with Him.

In his second speech (Job 34), Elihu will defend the justice of God by declaring how God handles everyone on earth.

ᔓ Please pray for the Holy Spirit to give you understanding of God's Word. ᔓ

Please read Job 34:1-37.

What does Elihu want his listeners to do, according to Job 34:1-4?

In the verses below, what does Elihu say that Job has said?
Job 34:5-6

Job 34:9

Elihu summarizes what he has heard from Job and Eliphaz and puts words in Job's mouth. Job didn't actually say those things, but Elihu has accurately summarized Job's distorted view of God's justice. Just a reminder, in the lessons on Job's early speeches, we recognized that the extreme distress and despair and confusion caused this distortion. Elihu was right to confront Job about this.

But Elihu was wrong in his basic premise about Job, just as the other friends were wrong.

How did Elihu describe Job, according to Job 34:7 and Job 34:37?

*It's hard to sort out all the right and the wrong, isn't it? Elihu summarizes Job's attitude correctly but incorrectly declares Job a wicked sinner. It was right for Elihu to correct Job's false statements about God, but he does so with his limited assessment that Job was suffering due to sin. For all of his wisdom, he still didn't know the whole story. In his defense, Elihu did say that he was going to share his **opinion**! (Job 32:10, 17)*

Should we declare that we know God's purposes in a given situation, even when we declare biblical truth about God in that situation? If you share your opinion, how should you do it?

Let's look at what Elihu says about God. Remember, his initial summary statement about God is absolutely correct: "God is greater than man." (Job 33:12)

Complete the statements of truth below, based on Job 34:10-12.
God does no ________________________________.

The Almighty does not commit ________________________________.

God repays man according to ________________________________.

God will never ________________________________.

The Almighty will not ________________________________.

What are the answers to Elihu's rhetorical questions about God, noted below?
Job 34:13 "Who gave Him charge over the earth?" ____________________________

Job 34:13 "Who appointed Him over the whole world?" ________________________

Job 34:17 "Will you condemn Him who is most just?" ________________________________

Job 34:18 "Who says to a king, 'You are worthless?'" ________________________

Job 34:18 "Who says to nobles, 'You are wicked?'" __________________________

Elihu also asked, "Should one who hates justice govern?" (Job 34:17) This question demonstrated a logical impossibility and made the point that God rules supremely and His justice is perfect.

What is the right perspective about God's justice according to the points made in the two previous exercises?

How did Moses summarize God's justice and rule, according to Deuteronomy 32:3-4?

Because God is the ultimate and only authority over the world and all that is in it, what does He have the right to do if He wants to, according to the following verses?
Job 34:14-15

Job 34:19-20

God's omniscience (complete knowledge) and omnipresence (presence everywhere) are attributes that enable Him to do what, according to Job 34:21-28?

I am thankful for all these statements of truth about our God. One of the most comforting is that God "does not need to examine a person further." (Job 34:23) God knows me. He knows everything about me. I don't need to explain myself to Him. I need Him to explain me to me!

Take time to pray that your God, who knows you better than you know yourself, will give you His truth, instruction, encouragement, correction and direction . . . whatever you need, when you need it.

Elihu asks a critical question that speaks most appropriately to Job's situation. *The Holman Christian Study Bible* translates it best: But when God is silent, who can declare Him guilty? When He hides His face, who can see Him? Yet He watches over both individuals and nations, so that godless men should not rule or ensnare the people." Job 34:29-30

How does this apply to Job's suffering and his concerns and questions to God?

Though God remains silent, i.e., He lets affairs on earth take their ordinary course so that a tyrant rises to rule over a nation, who among mankind would ever be in a position to condemn him as Job has? (Job 24:1-17) When God hides his face (i.e. Himself) or seems to withdraw His influence from the course of events on earth, no one can behold Him. Then evil appears to reign supreme. Nevertheless, God is still in control over both a nation and a man . . . God's slowness to act does not deny His sovereignty.[85]

If God chooses to remain silent and hidden at any time, in any circumstance, He has the right to do so. Wow. And because God is greater than man, we have no right to criticize Him for His choice.

Are you experiencing any situations where God is remaining silent or hidden? How does the truth of Job 34:29 help you understand and/or accept this?

It is an extreme test of faith and obedience to endure trials and sufferings and silence from God. But He is faithful and watching.

In Psalm 13, David gives us an excellent example of how to pray during hard times. What are some of his statements that would be helpful for you to pray during a time of silence from God?

Let's finish up Elihu's second speech, looking at his concluding comments. As noted earlier in this lesson, Elihu is right to confront Job with his distorted view of God's justice, but he is wrong to think that Job is suffering due to sin.

What accurate and appropriate point does Elihu make about God as he challenges Job in Job 34:31-33?

You might have had to think about that one a little bit. God is free to carry out His justice on His own terms and is not required to respond to Job in the way that he thinks he deserves. Some commentators think that Elihu is instructing Job to confess his sin and repent in verses 31-32. But he does not suggest a prayer repentance; instead, Elihu is pointing out that Job (the "someone") is demanding that God tell him his specific sins. In verse 33, Elihu accurately points out that God does not have to answer Job according to Job's terms.

The last observation to make from this second speech of Elihu is how he described Job's words. It's important, because God will say the exact same thing to Job. What is the first phrase in Job 34:35?

Bluntly put, Elihu says Job didn't know what he was talking about. Job did know that he lived blamelessly, with integrity, fearing God; and turning from evil. Job did know that God is awesome and sovereign. But Job didn't know what he was talking about when he questioned God's justice.

Let us pray to know when we don't know and may our words be few at that time! When God is silent, it may be best for us to be silent as well.

Blessed be the Name of the Lord.

I'm happy to say that Elihu's words are fewer in his third speech, but he does make some powerful points. Let's take a brief look at Speech #3 now.

Please read Job 35:1-16, below.

Job 35:1HCSB Then Elihu continued, saying: [2]Do you think it is just when you say, "I am righteous before God"? [3]For you ask, "What does it profit You,[1] and what benefit comes to me, if I do not sin?" [4]I will answer you and your friends with you. [5]Look at the heavens and see; gaze at the clouds high above you. [6]If you sin, how does it affect God? If you multiply your transgressions, what does it do to Him? [7]If you are righteous, what do you give Him, or what does He receive from your hand? [8]Your wickedness affects a person like yourself, and your righteousness another human being. [9]*People cry out because of severe oppression; they shout for help from the arm of the mighty.* [10]*But no one asks, "Where is God my Maker, who provides us with songs in the night,* [11]*who gives us more understanding than the animals of the earth and makes us wiser than the birds of the sky?"* [12]*There they cry out, but He does not answer, because of the pride of evil men.* [13]*Indeed, God does not listen to empty cries, and the Almighty does not take note of it—* [14]how much less when you complain that you do not see Him, that your case is before Him and you are waiting for Him. [15]But now, because God's anger does not punish and He does not pay attention to transgression, [16]Job opens his mouth in vain and multiplies words without knowledge.

In Elihu's third speech, above, I have underlined several comments. What is Elihu repeating to Job that he has already communicated?

I have placed a box around a description of God's immutability—His unchangingness. Please summarize this in your own words.

While our actions do not affect changes in our God, they do affect others, as stated in Job 35:8. How might your sin impact another sinner's life? How might your Christlikeness impact another's life?

J. Vernon McGee tells the following story as an illustration to Job 35:8. He says: You are always a witness, my friend. You are a preacher, regardless of who you are. The mother of a drunken man asked me to talk to her son. Once when he went wobbling down the street, I detoured him into my study. I told him what a low-down, dirty ingrate he was and how he disgraced his mother, breaking her heart. He just sat there and took all of it. Then I said, "You preach by your life. You are a preacher." He stood up to fight me. I could call him anything in the world except a preacher. Well, my friend, you are a preacher! Your wickedness will hurt somebody, and your righteousness may help somebody. [86]

I have italicized several verses in the passage on the previous page and circled two words to show where "there" is. According to Elihu, when do people "cry out" ?

According to Elihu, these cries are not addressed to God (which is why he calls them "empty" in verse 13). How does he prove that they are not praying to God?

What wonderful truth and comforting description about God is given in these italicized verses? Try to make at least 3 statements about God.

Continue looking at the topic of prayer in the italicized verses. Why does Elihu say that God does not answer prayer?

It has been said by someone that "there are no atheists in foxholes," meaning that in the most dire circumstances people will pray to God for help. But Elihu makes the point that there are people who cry out in pain but still don't turn to God for His help. These cries are empty, not addressed to God; and He may choose not to respond to that cry. It's appropriate to remember a statement from Elihu's second speech: "But when God is silent, who can declare Him guilty?" Job 34:29[HCSB]

Here's a review of what we've learned about our awesome God from Elihu's speeches so far:

God is greater than man. Job 33:12
God does no evil. Job 34:10
God never perverts justice. Job 34:12
God is the supreme authority over the earth. Job 34:13
God is the most just. Job 34:17
God is not partial. Job 34:19
God is omniscient and omnipresent. Job 34:21-22
When God is silent, He is watching over both individuals and nations. Job 34:29
God carries out His justice on His own terms. Job 34:33
God is our Maker, gives us songs in the night, teaches us and makes us wise. Job 35:10

Blessed be the name of the Lord! He hears your praise, so take some time to worship Him now.

~Blessed be the Name of the Lord.~

Elihu has been an important player in the game. He made some mistakes, but he scored a lot of points presenting his exalted view of our sovereign God. He's still on the field; and he is still calling the plays, so we've got one more long speech of his to study in the next lesson. You won't want to miss it!

Lesson 30 ~ Job 36 and 37

ELIHU'S ZEAL FOR THE LORD

I've got so many emotions swirling in my thoughts right now about Elihu's last speech!! I've spent a lot of time reading and rereading it and looking at various translations and commentaries. One commentator said that some "loathe Elihu" . . . and while I can't bring myself to that attitude, I can see why someone would feel that way. He frustrates me but also leads me to delight in the wonder of God! I have to trust that God has allowed Elihu's words to be written in His eternal record, and that means they are profitable to us—as an example (maybe of what ***not*** *to do!), or as a rebuke, a correction, an instruction, or training in righteousness.*

What we've learned so far from Elihu is that he is really mad at Job and his friends; he is young but has a lot to say and is confident in his wisdom. He appropriately confronted Job for justifying himself instead of God, but he inappropriately accused Job of being a sinner whom God has disciplined. He has also defended the greatness of God, highlighting His supreme authority and perfect justice. All of this is going to continue in his fourth speech. It's another mix of very harsh words to Job and incredibly reverent words about God.

All scripture is inspired by God—so let's see what we can learn from Elihu's final speech.

Please pray for understanding of the Scriptures inspired by the Holy Spirit.

Please read Job 36:1 - 37:24.

What is Elihu's "thesis statement" for his whole speech—stated in Job 36:5 and repeated in conclusion in Job 37:23?

Elihu will prove that thesis with examples about God's dealing with the wicked and the righteous and with an example about God's dealing with the world through the weather. Elihu still emphasizes disciplinary suffering where God brings a sinner to repentance, but he also includes the idea of the retribution principle where the wicked are punished and the righteous are rewarded. And we will see Elihu deliver a guilty verdict upon Job: he is a sinner who needs to repent.

According to Elihu, how do the following behave and/or how does God deal with them?
The wicked (Job 36:8-9, 12)

The righteous (Job 36:7-12)

The godless in heart, a hypocrite (Job 36:13-14)

The afflicted (Job 36:15-16)

> His words contain veiled accusations against Job. One need not be too imaginative to see that the man who lived as a king but fell into a prison of darkness was Job himself. Following Elihu's logic, it only remains for Job to recognize his sin and await instruction from God. Like the three friends, moreover, Elihu becomes increasingly strident and intemperate in his choice of words. He declares that all the wicked will die among the male prostitutes of the shrines (36:14). Apparently Job's skin disease has suggested to him the sexually transmitted diseases these prostitutes may have had. Elihu, too, has become cruel in his attempt to bring Job into submission.[87]

According to Elihu, what is Job's situation and what does he need to do? See Job 36:17-21.

While the words of Elihu to Job are strong and scathing, he does make a valid point in the midst of his accusation. The ESV has a good translation of Job 36:18a: "Beware lest wrath entice you into scoffing." What an important warning this is. When we are suffering, we can easily slip into wrong reactions to our suffering. I know I do it. Anger. Complaint. Jealousy of other's lack of suffering. Scoffing at the truth. Job had mocked the justice of God by calling it into question. When I say, "that's not fair . . . ," or "I don't deserve this . . ." I do the same thing. Lord, forgive me please.

If we are to be careful not to mock the Lord or scoff at His truth during times of trial and suffering, what are we to do instead?

Do you need some reminders of what God's word tells us to do, whether we are suffering or not? Make a few notes from the references below:
Psalm 103:1-6

Ephesians 4:29-32

Philippians 4:4-8

May we walk worthy of our God at all times. Remember what we learned in the last lesson—we are all preachers!

Job 36:21 is Elihu's last direct admonishment to Job regarding his behavior in his suffering. There are many translations of this verse, but the one below by Elmer B. Smick in The Expositor's Bible Commentary makes so much sense in light of the prologue—where God pointed out Job to Satan as one who feared God and turned from evil.

Job 36:21: Beware of turning to evil, for that is why you are tested by affliction.

Satan has been allowed to test Job, doing all that he could to make him turn ***to*** *evil and curse God. Job has held fast his integrity and his faith even though he has questioned God's justice in his anguish.*

What do we need to remember about Satan's mission and his methods? (You may want to review some of your notes from Lesson 3.)

Remember that Satan is roaming the earth, as a lion looking for someone to devour and discredit God in the process. But Almighty God is always in control in the heavens and the earth!

Elihu is about to conclude his speech, and it will come with crashing thunder and lightning as he declares how our mighty God carries out His justice in the world. His illustration is directly pointed at Job to cause him to be in awe of how God works and to fear Him.

It seems like a good time to remember the meaning of the name of Elihu, the son of Barachel. Elihu: "He is my God." Barachel: "God blesses." He is my God and He blesses. Truth!

In the verses below, what rhetorical questions does Elihu pose to Job? What are the unspoken answers to them?

	Question	**Answer**
Job 36:22		
Job 36:23a		
Job 36:23b		

Instead of questioning God's work, what does Elihu say we are to do, according to Job 36:24?

And that's what Elihu is going to do. All of God's work is to be respected, whether He carries it out for punishment, correction, or blessing.

Why should we praise God and His work, according to Job 36:25-26?

In Job 36:27-31, what does God do that no one can truly understand?

It's all about thunder and lightning in Job 36:32–37:5. What is Elihu's point?

What is God's purpose in snow and rain and cold and ice and clouds, based on Job 37:6-13?

Elihu's purpose in bringing this to Job's attention is to show that "the mystery of God's ways in nature coincide with the mystery of His ways in providence."[88] *Just as it is impossible to completely understand all of God's ways with storms, it's also impossible to completely understand all of God's ways in the stormy sufferings of our lives.*

There is a very special word found in that beautiful purpose statement in Job 37:13. The NIV says, "He brings the clouds to punish men, or to water His earth and show His love."

Please look up the following word:
Love: Strong's #2617
Hebrew word:
Hebrew definition:

If you've studied the Bible with me before, you've seen that this is a very important word! It is translated differently in modern versions of the Bible because it is so rich in meaning: faithful love, love, mercy, lovingkindness, unfailing love. This special love of God is based on His covenant promises. Because the book of Job may be the very first book of the Bible ever written, this may be the first occurrence of this word. I suggest that God's faithful love here is based upon His covenant made with Noah – that He would never again destroy the earth by flood. So when the rains come down, to punish or to provide nourishment, we can trust that He keeps His promise and acts in faithful love.

After bringing attention to the awesome power of God, Elihu asks some questions to make Job think about his attitude towards God.

How does Elihu prepare Job for his questions? What does he say in Job 37:14?

I love this verse. While I do think that Elihu often speaks harshly to Job, here, I appreciate the direction that he gives Job's thoughts. No matter what our problem is—if we will stop and think about God, and Who He is, and what He has done, and what He can do and will do—we will get re-oriented in the right direction.

Stop thinking about yourself. Stop thinking about your problem. Start thinking about your God.

Let's see how you would answer Elihu's questions. Note your response and what the question prompts you to remember about God.

Job 37:15[NLT] Do you know how God controls the storm and causes the lightning to flash from his clouds?

Job 37:16[HCSB] Do you understand how the clouds float, those wonderful works of Him who has perfect knowledge?

Job 37:17-18[HCSB] You whose clothes get hot when the south wind brings calm to the land, can you help God spread out the skies as hard as a cast metal mirror?

When did God spread out the skies? At creation, of course. The Hebrew words used in this verse are related to the words used in Genesis 1:7-8: "So God made the expanse and separated the water under the expanse from the water above the expanse. And it was so. God called the expanse sky." HCSB The verb "spread out" in Job 37:18 could refer to the hammering out of metal to make a mirror; and the word "expanse" is based on the same root, which as a noun means a beaten metal plate and is understood as a solid dome, the firmament of the skies. In the ancient Near East, mirrors were made of beaten bronze rather than glass.

The last few statements of Elihu's speech emphasize the transcendent splendor of our God.

How does Elihu exalt the Lord in Job 37:20-23?

The majesty of God is overwhelming; and we should be in awe of Him. But Elihu "is mistaken in his assertion that God is beyond human reach . . . God is going to demonstrate that He is both beyond human reach (transcendent), yet accessible in His immanence."[89] God is about to show up and speak with Job. I think Elihu will be surprised!

In conclusion, Elihu says, "Therefore men fear Him; He does not regard any who are wise in their own conceit." Job 37:24 ESV He's right. But this wasn't news to Job. Here's what Job said not too long ago: "God alone understands the way to wisdom; He knows where it can be found, for He looks throughout the whole earth and sees everything under the heavens. He decided how hard the winds should blow and how much rain should fall. He made the laws for the rain and laid out a path for the lightning. Then He saw wisdom and evaluated it. He set it in place and examined it thoroughly." And this is what He says to all humanity: "The fear of the Lord is true wisdom; to forsake evil is real understanding." Job 28:23-28 NLT

Isn't that interesting? Did Elihu say anything Job didn't already know? It doesn't seem like it. But maybe Elihu's angry speech did make Job realize that he had justified himself rather than God. Job doesn't reply to him. We don't know why. But his silence gives us time to think.

When someone confronts you with a problem in your thinking, how do you respond?

Through his four speeches, Elihu has given all of us a warning—against thinking that our suffering allows us to challenge God for what He does and what He allows. He rebuked Job for thinking too much of himself, and we've been able to examine ourselves for that fault as well.

And now, finally, we can look forward to hearing the Lord Himself speak.

Thank You Lord for Your blessing of ____

____

Blessed be the Name of the Lord.

Lesson 31 ∾ Job 38, 39, 40, and 41

GOD SPEAKS

Job and his friends didn't know that the Lord would show up and speak. But we've been expecting Him. So without further ado, let us listen to our keynote speaker, who needs no introduction.

I want to give you time to read through God's speech at your own pace. I will leave the rest of this page blank, for you to make notes, or jot down questions, or just respond in worship to your awesome God.

∾ Please pray for the Holy Spirit to give you understanding of God's Word. ∾

Please read Job 38:1 – 41:34.

Our God is magnificent, is He not? In His grace, He has shown up to speak to Job and show him how to be rightly related to His God. That's what He does all the time! It is important that we study these words of Scripture as we are to study all Scripture—to understand what the author meant when he wrote it. We need to study what God has said to Job in the context of the book of Job, as well as in the context of the whole Bible. I am so thankful that we can read the words of the Lord on this side of the cross with enlightenment from the Holy Spirit.

The Lord introduces His speech and His intentions clearly. Let's make sure that we begin our study of His words according to His purpose.

What did Job say he wanted and what was his attitude, in Job 31:35-37?

What did the narrator make clear in Job 38:1?

Please look up the definition for the following word:
Answer: Strong's #H6030
Hebrew word:
Hebrew definition:

This is a simple word, and it's been used at the beginning of every speech. It's such a normal part of our language that it almost doesn't seem important. But we should read this word in Job 38:1 as if it were written in capital Hebrew letters! What Job has been crying out for, begging for, and even demanding of God is now happening. If Eliphaz, Bildad, Zophar, and Elihu are still around, they must be in shock because they have tried to convince Job that there is no way God would answer him.

What did David know and say in Psalm 17:6?

What do we know according to Hebrews 4:16?

We have seen through our study of Job that God is sovereign and will do what is right. He knows when to remain silent and when to speak. There have been long periods of silence from the Lord – when the Israelites were oppressed in Egypt for 400 years and before the birth of Christ there were 400 years without a spoken revelation from Him.

And then—God not only spoke, but He spoke, in person. He came to earth, in human form, as Jesus. Emmanuel. God with us. It is amazing that God showed up and spoke to Job. It is even more amazing that God Himself came to earth in the form of a man and spoke to us. I am overwhelmed as I think on this truth.

Please read the words Jesus spoke which are recorded in John 8:23-28.

What is God's ultimate concern for us according to John 8:24?

God always speaks to us for our good. From His first words to Adam through His last recorded words in the book of Revelation, His words are for our good and His glory. Not one word of His is wasted. Every word is pure and perfect and wise and trustworthy. He wants us to know Him as He is and relate to Him, to fellowship with Him as He deserves.

With this in mind, God answered Job.

According to Job 38:1, He presented Himself and spoke through the ___________________.

A dark, ominous, blowing wind. A storm. The Old Testament tells us that God has manifested Himself this way a few times (Psalm 83:15; Isaiah 29:6; Jeremiah 23:19; Ezekiel 1:4). It is often an indication of His wrath and judgment on people. I'll admit that it's very hard for me to say that God is showing up and speaking to Job in anger. But, it's true. Job is in trouble!

All four friends have explained their version of Job's problem. Now, God makes it clear. How does the Lord describe Job's perspective about his suffering, according to Job 38:2?

"Darkened" means to be dark, black, dim, hidden, obscure. "Counsel" means purpose, plan. The Lord clearly confronts and rebukes Job for hiding His purpose for Job's suffering by talking about something he didn't understand at all.

Because we know the "backstory" of Job's suffering (Job 1–2), this should make sense to us. Explain what God was communicating to Job in your own words.

Is it possible for us to obscure God's purposes today by words spoken without understanding? How can we try to avoid this?

Where should we find understanding about the things of God, based on 1 Corinthians 2:9-13?

As we study the things of God, the ways and wisdom of God as He describes them Himself in His speech to Job, may we depend on the Holy Spirit to give us the understanding and application that we need. May we delight in, be instructed by, and be humbled by the sacred words of our wise Creator.

The answer to Job's problems was not an *explanation about God*, such as the three friends and Elihu had given, but a *revelation of God.* [90]

Thank You Lord for Your blessing of ____

____

ᔓBlessed be the Name of the Lord.ᔓ

Lesson 32 ᔓ Job 38

THE LORD ASKS JOB

The Lord knows ***exactly*** *what to say, when to say it, and how to say it. Always! He may whisper, as He did to Elijah (1 Kings 19:12-13). He may sing joyfully as He delights in His people (Zephaniah 3:17). He may thunder as He did against the Philistines one day (1 Samuel 7:10). He speaks with promises, blessings, warnings, and commands. And He asks questions—not because He needs to know the answer, but because* ***we*** *need to know and acknowledge the answer.*

And so He spoke to Job out of the whirlwind and asked, "Who is this who obscures My counsel with ignorant words? Get ready to answer Me like a man; when I question you, you will inform Me." Job 38:2-3 [HCSB]

Answer like a man . . . that put Job in his place right from the start. Job was just a man. A created being, not the Creator. The Lord God Almighty is about to reprove Job by bringing his limited wisdom and ability to his attention. Everything God asks Job about is an amazing, yet a simple activity for Him! Nothing is too difficult for God!

According to Job 38:4-11:
What are the first activities that God asks Job to tell Him about?

If Job were to answer these questions, what should he say?

What does Genesis 1:9-10 say that God did?

Let it be. And so it was. And it was good. Not too hard for God! John Wesley said, "He created all there is and He didn't even half try."

Just a sidenote: There are stories of mythological gods being at war with the sea and finally vanquishing its chaos. Marduk (the god) fights Tiamat (the sea) according to Mesopotamian mythology, and Baal (the god) fights Yam (the sea) in territories around Canaan. Remember, when you take the true God out of the picture, you lose the truth.

Debunking the myths, God tells Job that He handled the sea as His own newborn child, clothing it, swaddling it, and teaching it where it could and could not go.

What exciting thing happened at creation, according to Job 38:7?

Do you remember when we first heard about the "sons of God"? It was in Job 1, when they came to present themselves before the Lord. We learned that they are angels, and that's also what "morning stars" are referencing. The angels were watching God create the heavens and the earth, and they gave Him an enthusiastic acclamation! One angel, however, sometimes referred to as a "star of the morning" fell from heaven because of his pride (Isa.14:12-13). We don't know whether that was before creation or after; but by the time God spoke about this to Job, Satan was no longer singing for joy about anything God did.

The Lord also asked Job:

Have you ever commanded the morning to appear and caused the dawn to rise in the east? Have you made daylight spread to the ends of the earth, to bring an end to the night's wickedness? As the light approaches, the earth takes shape like clay pressed beneath a seal; it is robed in brilliant colors. The light disturbs the wicked and stops the arm that is raised in violence. **Job 38:12-15** NLT

How many times had Job done what is described in the verses above? What about God?

Can you describe a morning sunrise that caused you to be in awe of God?

Consider Job's discussions with his friends. Why is it meaningful that God mentions the wicked in the verses above?

Job has been questioning God's justice. God just mentions that—oh, by the way—He deals with the wicked every day.

There's a book entitled 1000 Places to See Before You Die: A Traveler's Life List. It includes brief descriptions of what it considers the world's wonders.

What mysterious places can only God visit, listed in Job 38:16-22? Has Job been to any of them? Does he answer God?

Regarding the depths of the sea and the gates of death:

God proceeded to question Job about the subterranean waters under the earth. Have you journeyed to the springs of the sea beneath the earth's surface or walked in the recesses of the deep? Such acts were beyond Job's ability to perform. Have the gates of death been shown to you? Job did not know what awaited man following death. Thus, his comments about death [during his earlier speeches] were spoken in ignorance. Such knowledge was inaccessible to Job.[91]

What about today? The Pacific Ocean has been measured as deep as 35,810 feet or 6.78 miles, and the Voyager 2 spent twelve years going 4.4 billion miles into outer space. Does our technology and ability to travel to deep and distant places give us wisdom and knowledge equal to that of God? Does medical technology that provides life-support to the terminally ill make us "all-knowing" in regards to life and death?

Does scientific knowledge give man everything there is to know? Why or why not?

How does God express His control over light and darkness in Job 38:19-20?

What does God say to Job to remind him of his lack of knowledge in Job 38:21?

Maybe at some point in your life you were told: "you're old enough to know better!" How old do you have to be to know better than God?

The Lord says that He has reserved hail for a time of trouble and a day of battle and war. Two occasions like this are described in the verses below. Note the circumstances.
Exodus 9:18 and 24

Joshua 10:11

How's the weather today? Can *The Weather Channel* do anything about it? Can Job control it? What do we learn from God's question in Job 38:24-30?

Who causes it to rain in the wilderness, where no one lives? What is God's purpose in that? I'm not questioning it as I bring it up. It's something God points out that He does. I don't really understand why He does it. I expect at this point in time there are scientists who can explain benefits of rain in desolate, uninhabited places. It's the whole ecosystem, I guess. But still—it was all God's idea in the first place!

Please read Genesis 1:11-19 and answer the questions below.
What did God do on the third day and what did He think about it?

What did God do on the fourth day and what was His purpose according to verse 14?

Highlight the phrases below that reflect God's purpose above.

Job 38:31-33 Can you bind the beautiful Pleiades? Can you loose the cords of Orion? Can you bring forth the constellations in their seasons or lead out the Bear with its cubs? Do you know the laws of the heavens? Can you set up God's dominion over the earth?

I've been studying these passages during the day, but at night I've stepped outside to look up and see the stars. Oh, the night sky is beautiful. I can only recognize the Big Dipper and Orion's Belt, but I've just learned from The Star Guide that the Big Dipper is a part of Ursa Major—the Great Bear! It represents the tail and hindquarters of the Bear. The Star Guide also says that "Orion fell in love with seven sisters, the Pleiades, and pursued them, as he does still in the heavens." It also says, "The Pleiades, or Seven Sisters is easily seen with the naked eye and looks glorious in binoculars. We can see up to seven stars in the [cluster] Pleiades with the naked eye, but binoculars or a small telescope will reveal that it consists of many more stars. Altogether it contains several hundred, and this number is typical of an open cluster."[92]

What do you think about the stars?

Just a few more questions to confound us today . . . and let's consider them as to what Job would say in response and what God would say if He were to answer His own question.

Job 38:34 Can you command the clouds so that a flood of water covers you?

Job would say: ____

God would say: ____

Job 38:35 Can you send out lightning bolts, and they go? Do they report to you: "Here we are"?

Job would say: ____

God would say: ____

Job 38:37 Who has the wisdom to number the clouds?

Job would say: ____

God would say:____

This verse has been fascinating me since I began studying the book of Job a year ago! I've looked up and thought of how impossible it is for me to count the clouds. They move and morph, and I can't pay attention long enough or count high enough anyway. As I studied these verses again, I looked at a book entitled Orbit: NASA Astronauts Photograph the Earth. It says, "John Glenn talked NASA into letting him carry a camera on the first United States flight into orbit, and no astronaut has been without a camera since." [93] *The book has spectacular photos from many space shuttle flights. From about 200 miles above the earth, the pictures taken looking down on the clouds make them look like nothing more than fluffy little cotton balls. God, in the heights of heaven, has the vantage point and capacity to count every cloud. To infinity and beyond!*

Job 38:37-38 Or who can tilt the water jars of heaven when the dust hardens like cast metal and the clods of dirt stick together?

Job would say: ____

God would say: ____

I left one question out of the set above. Job 38:36 is translated similarly in each of our recent versions of the Bible. The NIV says: "Who endowed the heart with wisdom or gave understanding to the mind?"

The words translated as heart and mind are rare Hebrew words and have uncertain meanings. One well-respected commentator leaves the words in the verses as they are: "Who put wisdom in tuhot? Who gave sekwi understanding?"[94] *Several options have been suggested by scholars including two intuitive birds—the ibis for tuhot and the rooster for sekwi. However, there is no agreement on the meaning of the two words.*

After much research and considering their comments myself, I have realized that whatever the meaning of the words may be, the question and answer remain the same . . . ***Who gave*** *the wisdom and understanding?* ***Who*** *actually knows the correct interpretation of the two mysterious words?! The mystery of the words just emphasizes our own limited knowledge today. Job would have understood God's example and acknowledged his finite wisdom before our incomprehensible God.*

As the Lord speaks, He refers to experiences and entities that would be very well-known to Job. Even the stars He refers to are some of the most well-known in the Northern Hemisphere and were recognized by ancient civilizations. And yet . . . for all our familiarity with sunrise and sunset, wind, rain, snow and stars . . . we cannot create or control them. Only God. Our God of wondrous works.

Thank You Lord for Your blessing of ____

____

Blessed be the Name of the Lord.

Lesson 33 Job 38:39 — 40:2

GOD'S WISDOM OVER HIS WILD KINGDOM

It's time to take a safari through God's animal kingdom. He will present to Job a few of His creations as examples of what He cares for and controls. God's wisdom and sovereignty are on display because even the wildest, most ferocious, untamable and strange creatures are dependent on the Lord.

Please pray for understanding of the Scriptures inspired by the Holy Spirit.

Please read Job 38:39 – 39:29 and make notes in the chart below.

Creature	Characteristics	God's Provision for it
Lion		
Raven		
Mountain Goat (possibly Nubian Ibex)		
Deer		
Wild Donkey (Swift Donkey, Onager)		
Wild Ox		
Ostrich		
Horse		
Hawk and Eagle		

While we might think this is a strange and very random list of creatures, they have certain things in common and the mention of one leads to next.

Lion and raven are connected by the concept of food; raven and ibex by their young; ibex and donkey by their free-ranging nature; donkey and ox by their untamable nature; ox and ostrich by their untrustworthiness; ostrich and horse by their relative speeds; horse and hawk by their senses from a distance; and, theoretically, hawk back to lion by their predation. [95]

If you have time and are interested in finding out more about these animals, do a little of your own research. Look at a Bible concordance and read other Scriptures that mention these animals. Search for information about them on the Internet! Make notes below from what you find.

What types of questions does God ask Job about these animals? What is God emphasizing to Job?

While we are considering the wild kingdom, I'd just like to mention a few of God's creatures that are especially near and dear to me and my family! I am fascinated with flamingos! I love that they are born grey, feed on shrimp, and turn pink as they mature. They are beautiful in a flock. They represent a variety of things to me: fun and fanciness; faith, hope and love; and resurrection. My husband delights in seeing what he calls "the winter cardinal." It's just a cardinal . . . but in the winter the male red bird stands out vividly in the midst of the grey and brown landscape. Why are sports teams named after that bird? Because it's very territorial. I've seen one male cardinal fight off another male cardinal at the bird feeder.

Speaking of red things, my daughter is just crazy about the red panda. I had never heard of it until a few years ago when it became her most favorite animal. It looks a little like a raccoon, is about the size of a house cat, but is related to the panda bear. Red pandas use their ringed tails as wraparound blankets in the chilly mountain heights. It is just one super cute little thing and is really fun to watch as it plays in the trees. (We've watched videos on YouTube!!) The Central Park Zoo has some on exhibit and seeing them in person was probably the highlight of my daughter's trip to New York City when she was 20 years old!

One more creature that I must mention is my daughter-in-law's favorite: the sea turtle! She says, "I think what I like about sea turtles is that they are very gentle and that even though they can be big, they are graceful swimmers. Some species are very beautiful with different patterns on their shells! I also find it very interesting that, like sharks and jellyfish, they have been around for a ***very*** *long time. What drew me to them was their nesting habits—the only time you can have interactions with sea turtles outside of the water is when the females are laying eggs at night or when the babies hatch. Although it's illegal to interact with sea turtles in the US without special permits, I've been lucky enough to participate in programs that allowed me to monitor their nests and see the baby turtles after they hatched!"*[96]

Which of God's creatures is your favorite, or the most intriguing to you, and why?

Let's go back and consider the animals God mentioned. The hungry lion and raven, the mountain goats and wild donkeys found in the wilderness, the untamable ox, the strange ostrich, the fearless horse, and birds of prey . . . were all mentioned as being beyond Job's control and understanding. If Job couldn't control God's animals, how could he think that he could control God?

What was God's question to conclude His first speech? See Job 40:1-2.

Based on this question, what was God's assessment of Job's response to his suffering?

Do you ever tell God that He is wrong about something? Do you try to correct Him? How might you have that attitude even if you don't use those words?

What was Job's response to the Lord's questions, based on Job 40:3-5?

We know that the book of Job became a part of the Israelites' scriptures. It's possible it was the text that was the foundation for many verses.

What is the wisdom found in Proverbs 30:32?

I have spoken once . . . and twice . . . but now . . . no more.

Job, the challenger, in a hand-over-mouth posture (v.4), realized how complex and mysterious God's ways were. In other words, the view of the things from God's perspective had chastened Job. His reply was based not so much on his unworthiness as on his insignificance. God had not crushed Job. God had not done what the counselors wanted when they reduced Job to zero, but he had cured Job's presumption. The Hebrew verb translated "unworthy" means "to be light" or "lightly esteemed" and in that sense "contemptible." Job saw how contemptible it must have appeared to God when he said "like a prince I would approach him" (31:37).[97]

In your own words, what was Job saying to the Lord?

What posture do you assume when you are humbling yourself before your awesome and holy God? What brings you to this point?

Job had been so moved by this experience, so taken out of himself by his vision of God, that he was released from his problem—his concern to be vindicated. And yet God had given him no explanation of his sufferings. He would no longer alternate outbursts of rage and self-pity. But he was still on the rack; suffering had not abated. Job had gone beyond it to see and trust God as his friend. As a friend God had brought Job out of his bitterness to a full realization that he must reckon with God as God. And yet Job still did not know how God had put Himself on trial when He allowed Job to be afflicted under Satan's instigation. So Job was humbled and thereby prepared for the Lord's second speech, which will pull together some important threads and bring the drama to a climax.[98]

What is most meaningful to you in the previous paragraph?

Our lesson today has shown us that Job realized that he had said so much more than he should have. But God knows that Job hasn't been completely broken. The really challenging and convicting questions are coming up next.

Thank You Lord for Your blessing of ____

____

ᔓBlessed be the Name of the Lord.ᔓ

Lesson 34 ᔓ Job 40:1-14

CONVICTING QUESTIONS

As we noted at the end of our last lesson, Job had been humbled, but not completely broken. The Lord knew it, even if Job didn't know it yet. So the Lord will continue to speak with Job to bring him to his senses and to a proper fear of God. I am so thankful that the Lord engages in communication with us to bring us to a right perspective of Who He is and who we are. I am so encouraged that the Lord knows me better than I know myself, and He will do what it takes to sanctify me.

What is God's ultimate purpose and plan for us, according to Romans 8:28-31?

God was definitely ***for*** *Job! He had commended him before Satan, protected him from death, and showed up "in person" to speak to Job for his good. The Lord's questions to Job were tough, but they came from love. God always works all things together for our good and for His glory.*

ᔓ Please pray for understanding of the Scriptures inspired by the Holy Spirit. ᔓ

Please read Job 40:1-14.

Please note each of the Lord's questions to Job below. Then in your own words, explain how Job's thoughts and attitudes needed adjusting. What was God pointing out to Job?

	Convicting Questions	**Attitude Adjustment**
Job 40:8(a)		
Job 40:8(b)		
Job 40:9(a)		
Job 40:9(b)		

Job had been accusing God of injustice because he felt that God had not been running the world the way he thought it should be run. Oh boy. Can you imagine thinking that about God? Well, I am realizing that I can be very Job-like when I question circumstances and wonder why God is letting something happen that doesn't seem right to me. Yikes.

I know it's wrong to question God and tell Him that He's doing something wrong. However, it's easy to complain about things. It's so easy to be angry at circumstances and trials and things not going my way. It's okay to grumble and whine and moan and protest about whatever is bothering me. Right? Uh-oh. I'm convicted.

What does Philippians 2:12-15 say?

If you complain about your circumstances, what does that indicate that you believe about God?

What does 1 Peter 4:19 say?

Peter connected God's creative power to assurance and hope in suffering. Our hope in suffering is literally bound up in the truth that God is the Creator of heaven and earth and everything and everyone in them. When you are having trouble with the **plan** of God, take time to notice the **power** of God in creation. [99]

Ah Lord God, please give me Your perspective on my life and whatever You allow in it. Please remind me to trust Your justice and Your mercy. Please remind me that You are God and I am not. I yield myself to the control of Your Holy Spirit so that I may walk in obedience to You and in kindness and patience and self-control with others. Amen.

I need to pause and pray. Do you?

God's next instructions to Job are going to help him see that he had a "God-complex" and had been talking as if he could handle the judgment of the wicked better than God.

Note below what God challenges Job to do. And in your own words, explain how Job's thoughts and attitudes needed adjusting. What should Job acknowledge?

	God's Challenge	**Attitude Adjustment**
Job 40:10		
Job 40:11		
Job 40:12		
Job 40:13		

God lays down the gauntlet. Go ahead Job. Do it. You think you can rule the world? Go ahead. Just try. "Then I myself will acknowledge to you that your own right hand can save you." Job 40:14 [NET]

It might seem surprising that God would say what is quoted above. But it's not a humbling of Himself or opening the door of possibility that Job might be able to do what he has been challenged to do. God laid down an overwhelmingly bold "double-dog-dare-you" dare, not as a bully, but as the One True Omnipotent and Wise God.

Is there anything that you can do that demonstrates that "your own right hand can save you"? Can you manage your own life better than God can? Can you protect yourself from evil? Can you do what it takes to enter heaven? Can you save yourself from an eternity of hell?

Please rejoice in this reminder from Scripture and write out the truth below.
1 Timothy 1:15

God alone can save us. He graciously provided a way for salvation through His Son Jesus Christ. It's a good time to remember that God's greatest good and greatest glory came through the worst suffering any man could ever experience. It was the worst possible suffering imaginable for the God-Man Jesus.

Who would have thought that it would be wise for God to send His one and only Son to earth, to suffer, be rejected, be condemned as guilty although He was innocent, and be executed in the most horrific way of crucifixion?

Who would have thought that God in the flesh would allow Himself to be killed?

Who would have thought that His death wouldn't be the end, but the beginning . . . of resurrection from the dead!

Hallelujah, Christ is risen! He is risen indeed! Job knew that his Redeemer—his God—his Savior—lived and that he would see him one day (Job 19:25)! Jesus saves!

Please review the verses below and note what they say regarding Job's perspective:
Job 32:2

Job 33:8-10

Job 34:5-6

Job 40:2

Job 40:8

How would you summarize Job's problem?

Job suffered. He didn't know why. He knew it wasn't because of some sin or hypocrisy. So he justified himself—he made himself the one who was right and God the one who was wrong. And that was wrong! Now please consider the idea of justification. It's one of those big theological words that is really wonderful but not really always understood. Justification, according to God's Word, means: the act of making something right, putting someone into a right relationship with God. Its meaning includes the idea of acquittal—found not guilty of sin.

Using two different colors, please highlight (1) phrases including the words "righteousness" and (2) phrases including the words just / justified / justifier / justification.

Romans 3:21-26ESV But now the righteousness of God has been manifested apart from the law, although the Law and the Prophets bear witness to it — [22]the righteousness of God through faith in Jesus Christ for all who believe. For there is no distinction: [23]for all have sinned and fall short of the glory of God, [24]and are justified by His grace as a gift, through the redemption that is in Christ Jesus, [25]whom God put forward as a propitiation by His blood, to be received by faith. This was to show God's righteousness, because in His divine forbearance He had passed over former sins. [26]It was to show His righteousness at the present time, so that He might be just and the justifier of the one who has faith in Jesus.

Romans 5:1-9ESV Therefore, since we have been justified by faith, we have peace with God through our Lord Jesus Christ. [2]Through Him we have also obtained access by faith into this grace in which we stand, and we rejoice in hope of the glory of God. [3]More than that, we rejoice in our sufferings, knowing that suffering produces endurance, [4]and endurance produces character, and character produces hope, [5]and hope does not put us to shame, because God's love has been poured into our hearts through the Holy Spirit who has been given to us. [6]For while we were still weak, at the right time Christ died for the ungodly. [7]For one will scarcely die for a righteous person — though perhaps for a good person one would dare even to die — [8]but God shows His love for us in that while we were still sinners, Christ died for us. [9]Since, therefore, we have now been justified by His blood, much more shall we be saved by Him from the wrath of God.

Romans 5:17-18ESV If, because of one man's trespass, death reigned through that one man, much more will those who receive the abundance of grace and the free gift of righteousness reign in life through the one man Jesus Christ. [18]Therefore, as one trespass led to condemnation for all men, so one act of righteousness leads to justification and life for all men.

Philippians 3:8-10ESV Indeed, I count everything as loss because of the surpassing worth of knowing Christ Jesus my Lord. For His sake I have suffered the loss of all things and count them as rubbish, in order that I may gain Christ [9]and be found in Him, not having a righteousness of my own that comes from the law, but that which comes through faith in Christ, the righteousness from God that depends on faith — [10]that I may know Him and the power of His resurrection, and may share His sufferings, becoming like Him in His death

2 Corinthians 5:21ESV For our sake He made Him to be sin who knew no sin, so that in Him we might become the righteousness of God.

Based on the truths above, regarding justification and righteousness, please summarize how God justified us and made us right with Him.

Isn't it fascinating that in this book of great suffering, we see one man making himself right and making God wrong. Then compare that to the man Jesus Christ, who endured the greatest suffering, who was God, who was right and made Himself "wrong" (taking on our sins), so that we could be "right" (forgiven of sin and reconciled to God).

Job made himself right and God wrong. God made Himself wrong and us right – through Christ. That is a mystery beyond all understanding.

Please read Job 40:1-14 once more. What has impacted you the most from these convicting questions and challenges from God to Job?

May convicting questions from the Lord always lead us to humility before Him and thankfulness that He has justified us in Christ.

Thank You Lord for Your blessing of ____

____

~Blessed be the Name of the Lord.~

Lesson 35 ~ Job 40:15 -24

THE MONSTER IN THE MARSH

Behold now! God tells Job to take a good look at one of His really incredible creatures. Behold... the BEHEMOTH!

What is a Behemoth? Speculations abound as to what animal this is. The Merriam-Webster Dictionary defines the word as: something very big and powerful, (1) a mighty animal described in Job 40:15-24 as an example of the power of God (2) something of monstrous size, power or appearance, i.e. a behemoth truck. [100]

I gave you the definition from a modern dictionary just to show you that this word is so well known that it is not only the name of an animal but has also become a very common adjective to describe something that is overwhelmingly huge and powerful.

Let's see what God wants us to behold about His Behemoth.

ᔓ Please pray for understanding of the Scriptures inspired by the Holy Spirit. ᔓ

Please read Job 40:15-24.

Briefly list every characteristic mentioned about this animal. I think you'll see a minimum of 14 details or perhaps a few more depending on your translations.

What does God say about His control over this huge and powerful creature?

Now let's try to understand why God has brought it to Job's attention. What would happen in the following "match-ups"?

God vs. Behemoth		Job vs. Behemoth
	Who is more powerful?	
	Who takes control?	
	Which is Creator or creature?	
	Who knows its purpose?	
	Who provides food?	

Behold now the Behemoth! Let's take some time to consider what this animal may be.

Do you see any statements in Job 40:15-24 which indicate that the Behemoth is a real animal? Briefly note your answer.

The Hebrew word "behemoth" is the plural form of the word "behemah" which is translated as beast or wild animal throughout the Scriptures, except in Job 40:15. There are only 11 verses where the Hebrew word "behemoth" is used (Deut. 32:24; Job 12:7, 40:15; Ps.8:7, 50:10, 73:22; Isa.30:6; Jer.12:4; Joel 1:20, 2:22; Hab.2:17); two of them are in Job. It is translated as "beasts" in Job 12:7, but remains as Behemoth in Job 40:15.

The reason that the word Behemoth remains mysterious and untranslated in the book of Job is because of the grammar used and the details given about this creature. As mentioned above, Behemoth is a plural word, but all the verbs and pronouns used in Job 40:15-24 are singular. The plural ending, therefore, has "an intensive force meaning the beast par excellence; that is, the beast becomes a monster." The singular verbs and pronouns indicate that one particular animal is being referred to, not many different animals.

Also adding to the mystery of the Behemoth is that the creature is clearly presented to Job by God as an example of a mighty, unconquerable animal. So what was the Behemoth? What animal completely fits the description given? My understanding of the text makes me believe that it was a real animal. Biblical scholars differ on their views of whether it was real or not, and if real, what animal it could have been. The hippopotamus, elephant, rhinoceros, and crocodile have all been proposed. Some see it as a mythological creature that would have been known through ancient civilizations' epic stories about their gods.

At this point in our study, what's your personal opinion about what the Behemoth was?

Here's another perspective:

If we take extinct animals into consideration, a herbivorous dinosaur seems a more likely candidate. The apatosaur had a large tail, lived on green plants and weighed about 30 metric tons.* The ultrasaur could reach a height of 18 meters* and a length of 30 meters, with a weight of 136 metric tons. It also was a herbivore with an enormous tail. The brachiosaur was 12 meters tall, 23 meters long and 60 to 70 metric tons in weight. Its tail could reach a length of nearly 6 meters and a breadth of nearly 1.5 meters. In the sauropods, large bundles of muscles are visible on the outside of the body of the animal. Behemoth is not only a herbivore, but more specifically it is a grass-eater. An animal that does fit this aspect is the 15 meters long nigersaur, found in the Republic of Niger in Africa. Because new kinds of extinct animals continue to be found in our time, and because the description in Job 40 is not specific enough, we cannot identify precisely which animal is described. [101]

*metric ton = 2204.6 pounds, meter = 39 3/8 inches

While we haven't studied the Leviathan yet, it too is as mysterious as the Behemoth and Professor Mart-Jan Paul refers to them both in his comments below:

Behemoth and Leviathan may well be now extinct species that were still living in Job's day. While what is known about several species of dinosaurs may appear to fit some aspects of God's description of Behemoth and Leviathan, the most we can say with confidence is that the descriptions do not match any known living species today. At the same time, to call them "mythological" creatures is to do violence to the text and context of Job; therefore, we affirm that these were actual creatures of which Job had knowledge (although we cannot state whether Job had direct or indirect knowledge of them). They symbolize the power of evil, connected with Satan, who is mentioned in the first chapters of the book. The words of God humbled Job and showed him that God is above all powers in this world.[102]

So many possibilities to consider! But what is most important? Please remember that the mysterious Behemoth is "hidden" in the middle of God's speech and God is humbling Job. He has pointed out to Job that he can't command the everyday occurrences of sunrise, sunset, and weather; he can't count the clouds and control the seasons; and he can't care for the wild animals of the wilderness.

Please read Job 40:6-24.

What challenge did God propose to Job in verse 11-13 and how might this relate to His mention of Behemoth?

If Job can't conquer the monumental Behemoth, then Job can't contend with God.

Now let's compare the following "match-up".

GOD	VERSUS	JOB
	More powerful	
	Takes control	
	Creator or creature	
	Knows its purpose	
	Provides food	

After studying and considering the context and the controversy surrounding Behemoth, I paused and reflected on what I should learn from this part of God's speech. I wondered . . . what is the "Behemoth" in my life? What is the biggest, strangest, most challenging, uncontrollable thing in my life right now? There's always something that is beyond my control.

What about you? What do you need to realize is the "Behemoth" in your life that only God can handle?

The bottom line in all our circumstances is trusting God. It's easy to say, but we are sometimes quite slow to do it. In Psalm 73, the psalmist Asaph expressed his slowness to trust God, but realized the truth about Him that he chose to cling to and trust. We've looked at this psalm before; it has many references to verses throughout the book of Job, and even uses the word behemoth in verse 22 where it is translated as "beast." If you have time, read the whole psalm, then answer the questions on the next page.

According to Psalm 73:21-28:
What was the psalmist's wrong attitude?

What behavior was like that of a beast?

What was the truth that he realized and clung to?

When horrible, confusing, challenging circumstances, tests, and trials come upon us, may we see them as the Behemoth under God's control, rather than acting like a monstrous behemoth in resistance to Him.

Thank You Lord for Your blessing of ____

____

~Blessed be the Name of the Lord.~

Lesson 36 ~ Job 41

A CREATURE UNDER GOD'S CONTROL

In this great book of mysteries and unanswered questions, it's time to study and consider God's presentation of His Leviathan—another intriguing, incomparable creature. It is fascinating that the Lord ends His lesson with a very long description of this wild, prideful "king." It is the closing example of what is overwhelming and undefeatable for man but no match for God. Job is no match for Leviathan, but Leviathan is no match for God. There are two applications for Job: he doesn't have the wisdom and power to fight with Leviathan or God, and God does have the wisdom and power to control Leviathan as well as anything and everything that happens to Job.

~ Please pray for understanding of the Scriptures inspired by the Holy Spirit. ~

Please read Job 41:1-33.

Job would have immediately recognized this creature by its name but we need to know more about it.

Based on verses 1, 7, and 31-32, where does Leviathan live?

What are the physical features of Leviathan based on the following verses?
Job 41:7

Job 41:12

Job 41:13

Job 41:14

Job 41:15-17

Job 41:18-21

Job 41:22

Job 41:23

Job 41:30

How do the following verses describe that it is undefeatable, untamable, and ferocious?
Job 41:1-10

Job 41:26-29

Job 41:33

The most complete description of Leviathan comes from Job 41 and includes these observations: It lived in the sea but sometimes came on shore, had a scaly hide that deflected spears, was huge and terrifying, breathed fire, left luminescent wakes, and had a neck, nose, and a mouth with terrorizing teeth. From Psalm 104 we learn that Leviathan played around in ancient shipping lanes.

These historical hints from the Bible refute the idea that Leviathan was a mythical creature that was being used as a literary metaphor. Metaphors don't deflect spears or scare the daylights out of onlookers. In fact, Leviathan must have really done these things for God to meaningfully compare it to His own might. Identifying Leviathan as a myth smuggles in the destructive idea that anything in Scripture could be interpreted as a myth. But since the Bible has proven itself true over centuries of scrutiny, the Leviathan must have really lived. [103]

While Leviathan is an incredible creature, the Lord doesn't talk about it just to have something interesting to say. Why did God talk about Leviathan?

What does God emphasize to Job in verses 9–11? Explain God's message to Job in your own words.

As we consider God's purpose in using Leviathan as an example of that which is under His control, please look at the other references to Leviathan in Scripture.

What do the following verses tell you about Leviathan?
Job 3:8

Psalm 74:13-14

Psalm 104:24-27

Isaiah 27:1

Leviathan was a real animal, now extinct. Undoubtedly in Job's world, it was the largest and fiercest of all the beasts that lived in or near the water. Imagine: God concluded His tour of the animal world with a dragon—a fire-breathing, unstoppable, untamable, fierce and fearful dragon. Could it be (we do **not** know for certain) that God concludes with Leviathan simply because it is this animal, used throughout Scripture, that represents Satan? [104]

What do the following verses tell you about Satan, referred to as the dragon?
Revelation 12:3-4

Revelation 12:7-9

Revelation 20:1-3, 7-10

I do not know if Job caught the analogy; he may have lacked the revelation we have been afforded to reveal the last days of the dragon. But we can be confident that the great dragon who accused Job would have been listening to the conversation between God and Job. He would not have missed a single word of it. [105]

So, why would God choose to talk about these giant, fierce, fire-breathing animals? More than likely, because these animals—above all others—seemed uncontrollable, untamable, able to crush everything in their path. And yet, they were shown to be creations of God, the Tamer of Creation, whose power is greater than any creature—including Satan himself. All the powers and forces and creatures of heaven and hell are under God's control. [106]

Please read through God's statements about Leviathan in Job 41:1-34 once more. How might the last 2 verses allude to the character of Satan?

No matter what you think Leviathan was or represents, the example of the Leviathan is clearly the climax of God's speech—His final "answer" to Job. There is no doubt that the Lord humbles Job with the examples of His power and wisdom over all things. The Lord uses the Leviathan as an example not only to show Job his lack of power, but also to show him His wisdom, power, and control over the most violent and dangerous of His creatures.

By showing Job that he couldn't control Leviathan, the Lord taught Job that he couldn't control God. What types of actions, attitudes, or prayers might indicate that you are trying to control God?

How are God's power, wisdom, and greatness magnified as He presents the Leviathan?

We have come to the end of the Lord's answer to Job. Please take time to read through Job 38:1-41:34 once again. What stands out to you at this point in our study of His speech?

Our wise and powerful Lord has spoken. Let us respond humbly in worship.

Thank You Lord for Your blessing of ____

____

Blessed be the Name of the Lord.

Lesson 37 ᔓ Job 42:1-6

JOB RESPONDS

It's not complicated. After all the suffering, all the speeches, all the speculation . . . our Sovereign God has shown Job that the simple fact of the matter is that He is in control. And Job doesn't know as much as he thought he knew. We are about to see how Job reacted to the Lord's words of wisdom. It's not complicated, and it's the perspective that we need every day of our lives.

ᔓ Please pray for the Holy Spirit to give you understanding of God's Word. ᔓ

Please read Job 42:1-6.

How would you describe Job's response to the Lord?

What two things does Job say that he knows about the Lord in Job 42:2?

We know that the Lord never explained all the circumstances of Job's suffering to him. But here, in Job's response, Job speaks of what he does know: God is all-powerful and God's purpose is the only thing that matters. In stating these two ultimate truths, Job shows that he realizes that this is all he needs to know.

This truth is so critical for us to believe. We must depend on it and submit our lives to it. Please write Job 42:2 and expound upon it based on your own life circumstances. Make this a prayer and a declaration of submission and trust.

Faithful followers of God have declared this great truth in prayer and praise and trust throughout history. Perhaps they learned it from Job. David, Solomon, the prophets, and even Jesus yielded to God's plan God's way.

Please record what is stated in the verses below. Let this exercise emphasize the magnitude of acknowledging that God is God and we are not.

Psalm 135:6

Proverbs 19:21

Ecclesiastes 3:14

Isaiah 46:10

Jeremiah 32:17

Mark 14:36

What critical truth did Job realize about himself according to Job 42:3?

Job had questioned the equity and justice of God's dealings (7:20, 21:7-34). God's wise handling of the physical and natural worlds convinced him that, though he may have committed no overt sin, he had dabbled in questions beyond his understanding and experience. [107]

This was the beginning of Job's confession about the error of his ways. He agreed that he had obscured God's counsel.

God's counsel and ways are too wonderful for us to grasp.

Delightful. Pleasant. Lovely. Enjoyable. These words show up as synonyms for "wonderful," and they convey my sentiments when I use the word wonderful. But it is a word that means so much more. The Theological Word Dictionary of the Old Testament says that it refers to something "unusual, that which is beyond human capabilities, that which awakens astonishment in man."[108] Another set of synonyms more accurately conveys the idea of this word: Magnificent. Breathtaking. Amazing. Astonishing. Extraordinary. Marvelous.

God's power is so great and His wisdom is so incredible that we can only consider it with wonder and awe. We cannot explain how He does what He does, and we may not be able to grasp why He does what He does.

What is wonderful, according to the following verses?

Psalm 119:18

Psalm 139:1-6

Psalm 145:5

Isaiah 9:6

Isaiah 28:29

Matthew 21:14-15

How did Job respond to God's merciful questioning, according to Job 42:4-6?

The Lord told Job to listen to Him; and when Job did so, he was able to hear about God from God Himself, whereas previously, he had only heard about God from others. It is very good to hear about our Lord from others, but we must know Him and hear Him through a personal, intimate relationship with Him ourselves.

What his **eyes had seen** of God refers not to a physical vision, such as a theophany, but to spiritual insight. Job now had a greater understanding of God's awesome character than before his suffering began. In this sense his agonizing trial had been worth the suffering. His eternal, spiritual gain outweighed his temporal, physical loss. [109]

How do you pursue an intimate relationship with the Lord in your daily life?

Have you experienced a time of suffering that you can say was worth the pain because you came to know and understand the Lord in a deeper way as a result?

The final words of Job recorded in his book according to the New Living Translation are: "I take back everything I said, and I sit in dust and ashes to show my repentance." Job 42:6

Thank you, Job, for humbling yourself and for showing us how to do it too.

Job did not need to repent over sins that brought on his suffering since his suffering was not the result of his sin. One should not, however, assume that Job had nothing to be sorry for. His questioning of God's justice, for which God chided him in 38:2 (quoted in v.3), is enough to call forth a change of heart and mind. [110]

Please take time to humble yourself before the Lord. Ask Him to make you aware of any areas in which you may be challenging His authority, wisdom, power, or plans. Pray for a change of heart and a new direction; and then enjoy the Lord's fellowship, comfort, and joy.

Psalm 19 tells of knowing God through His wonderful creation as well as through His wonderful word, and also leads us to humble ourselves before the Lord so that we are not led astray by unintentional or willful sins. This psalm sounds like it could have been inspired by the reading of Job 38—42. Please close today by reading and praying through this psalm.

Psalm 19:1-14[HCSB]

The heavens declare the glory of God, and the sky proclaims the work of His hands.
[2]Day after day they pour out speech; night after night they communicate knowledge.
[13]There is no speech; there are no words; their voice is not heard.
[4]Their message has gone out to all the earth,
and their words to the ends of the inhabited world.
[a]In the heavens He has pitched a tent for the sun.
[5]It is like a groom coming from the bridal chamber;
it rejoices like an athlete running a course.
[6]It rises from one end of the heavens and circles to their other end;
nothing is hidden from its heat.
[7]The instruction of the LORD is perfect, reviving the soul;
the testimony of the LORD is trustworthy, making the inexperienced wise.
[8]The precepts of the LORD are right, making the heart glad;
the commandment of the LORD is radiant, making the eyes light up.
[9]The fear of the LORD is pure, enduring forever;
the ordinances of the LORD are reliable and altogether righteous.
[10]They are more desirable than gold — than an abundance of pure gold;
and sweeter than honey — than honey dripping from the comb.
[11]In addition, Your servant is warned by them; there is great reward in keeping them.
[12]Who perceives his unintentional sins? Cleanse me from my hidden faults.
[13] Moreover, keep Your servant from willful sins; do not let them rule over me.
Then I will be innocent, and cleansed from blatant rebellion.
[14]May the words of my mouth and the meditation of my heart be acceptable to You,
LORD, my Rock and my Redeemer.

Blessed be the Name of the Lord.

Lesson 38 ∾ Job 42:7-10

THE REST OF THE STORY

Cliffhanger endings. Unsolved mysteries. Dramas . . . to be continued. Aren't you glad we don't have that in the book of Job? The author of this book of the Bible gave us the epilogue to bring all things to God's good conclusion. Just as he set the stage at the beginning of the book, he now tells us . . . the rest of the story. The details given are as specific as all the details throughout the book, which remind us that Job was a real man and this is a true account of a real event.

What happened after Job's one-on-one time with the Lord?

∾ Please pray for understanding of the Scriptures inspired by the Holy Spirit. ∾

Please read Job 42:7-17.

Now you know the whole story! We will end our study with two lessons on the epilogue.

What problem did Eliphaz and friends have and why, according to Job 42:7-9?

Job had said to his friends: "you coat the truth with lies; you are all worthless doctors." Job 13:4[HCSB] The Lord's words to Eliphaz indicated that Job's perspective was accurate.

The counselors certainly lacked the right information about why Job was suffering. Job spoke without understanding (v.3) and was often fiery and emotional in his remarks (15:12-13; 18:4). His opinions and feelings were often wrong, but his facts were right. He was not being punished for sins he had committed. But the friends were claiming to know for a certainty things they did not know and so were falsely accusing Job while mouthing beautiful words about God. Job rightly accused them of lying about him and trying to flatter God (13:4, 7-11).[111]

To summarize the friends' perspectives, fill in the blanks below by choosing the appropriate word from the following selection: **a) sin, b) justice, c) sovereignty, d) suffering.**

The friends believed in God's ________________, but they restricted God's _____________.

The friends declared that ___________was always and only a direct result of _____________.

What did the Lord require of Eliphaz, Bildad, and Zophar according to Job 42:7-9?

The number of bulls and rams required represented an enormous and expensive sacrifice. This shows the severity of their sin, which the Lord referred to as folly. While that word may indicate silliness to us today, according to its Biblical use, folly represents vile and disgraceful behavior. It also includes the actions of insulting God and having a mind closed to reason.

More than failing to comfort Job, they have tempted him to take the wrong course out of his affliction. Since their counsel would lead Job away from the true worship of Yahweh, they are accused of folly, the denial of God's goodness. The friends discourses, coming after his wife's foolish counsel, became Job's second temptation to curse God. Had he followed their exhortations, he would have denied God's faith in him by seeking God for his own personal gain.[112]

What did Eliphaz, Bildad, and Zophar realize about Job when the Lord told them to ask Job to offer sacrifices on their behalf and pray for them?

What special description did Lord give Job in Job 42:7-9? ? How many times did He repeat it?

This title suggests a close, bonded relationship and in the Old Testament is a title of honor for one who serves God. In His conversations with Satan, Yahweh referred to Job as His servant (1:8, 2:3). His use of this title again signifies that He has accepted Job's recantation and acknowledges that He has the same high status that he had prior to his trial. [113]

What did the Lord require of Job?

How was this similar to his actions on behalf of his children in Job 1:5?

We don't know what Job was thinking when the Lord told him to pray for his friends, but what attitudes may he have had to consider and possibly pray about for himself before praying for his friends?

What attitudes and behaviors do the following verses instruct you to have toward others?
Leviticus 19:16-18

Luke 6:27-38

Proverbs 25:18-20 describes a difficult person, but Proverbs 25:21-22 tells us what to do for him. How do these verses reflect Job and his friends?

What is the key to loving your neighbor, according to Galatians 5:13-16?

Is there anyone that you should pause and pray for right now?

Job 42:10 says: "after Job had prayed for his friends, the Lord restored his prosperity and doubled his previous possessions." Based on this verse, what was Job's situation when he prayed for his friends?

Does Job's prayerfulness, while still suffering, inspire you? Do you pray for others when you yourself are struggling in trials?

Read Job 42:1-10. Is there any indication that Job's actions were based on an expectation of reward or restoration of prosperity? Explain your answer.

Job was a man who was blameless and upright, fearing God and turning from evil. He worshipped the Lord for Who He is, not for what He gives. Job was the servant of the Lord for this reason, before, during, and after his suffering. May we pray like Job.

Thank You Lord for Your blessing of ____

____

Blessed be the Name of the Lord.

Lesson 39 ~ Job 42:10-17

P.S. JOB WAS BLESSED!

I'd like to write, "and they all lived happily ever after." And the end of the book of Job does make it sound like that is what happened. But there is so much more that we can learn from the final verses of this book. And there is no fairy tale ending to life on earth. The best is yet to come! Our hope must not be for a blissful existence in our mortal bodies, but for an eternity in heaven, face to face with God our Father and Jesus Christ our Savior. That will be our happy ever after!

The lessons we will learn from the end of the story of Job will help us take away the correct perspectives about our relationship with the Lord.

~ Please pray for the Holy Spirit to give you understanding of God's Word. ~

Please read Job 42:7-17.

We've considered so many heavy and hard subjects throughout this book. How would you describe the ending of Job?

"Indeed the LORD gave Job twice as much as he had before." Job 42:10[NKJV] Indeed! This word is so appropriate here, because there is a surprise in God's blessing of Job. He didn't ask for it. He didn't expect it. He didn't deserve it. The Lord just gave it. Generously.

We noticed in our previous lesson that the Lord commanded Job to pray for his friends while he was still in a situation of suffering. And we recognized that there was no indication that Job's circumstances would change as a result of his repentance before God or his prayers for his friends. Even though material blessings are nice, they are not to be our priority. There is something far better.

What was the very best situation for Job, according to Job 42:9?

Please let that sink in. The Lord accepted Job. Fellowship between Job and his God had been restored. Before his suffering, Job had known "days when God watched over me, when His lamp shone above my head, and I walked through darkness by His light!" He had enjoyed "days of my youth when God's friendship rested on my tent, when the Almighty was still with me." Job 29:2-5[HCSB] But after the loss of his children, livelihood, and health, he had experienced the silence of God. And then the Lord answered Job. And then Job knew Him face to face. And Job's self-righteousness was broken. He was humbled and knew the Lord better than he had ever known Him before. And the Lord accepted Job.

Did you notice that Job didn't do anything to deserve the acceptance of God? He only believed that God was Who He said He was; and Job humbled himself before God, repenting of his words spoken without knowledge. There was no requirement from the Lord for Job to gain acceptance, and there was no bargaining on Job's part for God to do something for him. The Lord called Job His servant before he prayed for his friends. God acted in grace toward Job.

Can you say "the Lord has accepted me"?

Please note how the following verses explain God's acceptance of you if you have trusted in Christ as your Savior:
Ephesians 1:3-4

Ephesians 1:11-12

Ephesians 2:4-5

Ephesians 2:8-9

Ephesians 2:17-19

The Lord demonstrated that He accepted Job by blessing him abundantly in a variety of ways. We've already seen that He blessed Job by hearing his prayer for his friends. Job's suffering had been publicly known, and now the Lord's favor on him would be shown to all as well.

According to Job 42:11, who came to the gathering at Job's house? Why did they come, and what did they bring?

During his suffering, Job had said, "My breath is repulsive to my wife; I am loathsome to my brothers. Even youngsters have scorned me; when I get up, they scoff at me. All my closest friends detest me; and those whom I love have turned against me." Job 19:17-19[NET]

Since all these people came to Job's house and ate with him and comforted him, what does this tell you about Job's attitude toward them?

Do unto others as the Lord has done unto you. Yes, I know, I've changed the Golden Rule a little bit; but I've stated a biblical truth.

How are Job's actions similar to the actions in the verses below?
Luke 7:44-48

Ephesians 5:1-2

Oh, let's celebrate the goodness of God! Let's do good to others because He has been good to us! Salvation, which is restoration of fellowship with our God, is the greatest blessing we can receive, and then to share God's grace and forgiveness and love to others is the best blessing we can give!

How do you like to demonstrate God's grace to others?

In the middle of the wonderful party at Job's house, the author of Job makes a deep, difficult statement. He says that the adversity Job experienced was brought upon him by the Lord. It would be nice to overlook this and keep enjoying the party, but it's too important to ignore.

How did the Lord Himself make a similar statement in Job 2:3?

How did Job make a similar statement in Job 2:10?

Can you accept these statements? Can you embrace the mystery of the sovereignty of God, who allows bad things to happen and who even inspired the author of this book to attribute Job's adversity to Himself? It's mind-boggling. Exactly! And that's what the Lord's speech to Job helped us realize. We don't understand all the ways and wisdom of the Lord.

I'd like to remind you of Job's humble perspective in response to the Lord's speech. Job answered the Lord, "I know that You can do all things; no purpose of Yours can be thwarted; You asked, 'Who is this who darkens counsel without knowledge?' But I have declared without understanding things too wonderful for me to know." Job 42:1-3[NET]

There are certainly ways of the Lord that are too wonderful, too mysterious for us to know. I hope that you can accept the mysteries of the Lord by faith and trust Him, even when you don't understand His ways. Let's look at a few verses that He has given us to comfort us during difficult days.

Please read the following truths found in the book of James, and write them out as prayers for yourself.

James 1:2-6

James 1:12-14

James 5:11

Ah! The Lord is kind, compassionate, merciful, and gracious! And to emphasize His acceptance of Job, He blessed him twice as much as before.

Look back to Lesson 2, page 17 for the list of Job's possessions before his suffering and note what he had before his suffering and what he had after his suffering according to Job 42:12.

He was previously called the greatest of all the men of the East! What would they call him now? Before his suffering, Job had seven sons and three daughters. After his suffering, the Lord blessed him with ten more children. Job's wife isn't mentioned in the epilogue; but we can be pretty sure she was around, don't you think? It's assumed that she was the mother of seven more sons and three more daughters. Commentators also mention that having these ten children would have doubled Job's offspring, because he would eventually be united with all twenty children in the presence of the Lord.

The blessing of the Lord was seen not only in the greatness of Job's possessions and in the strength of his seven sons, but also in the loveliness of his three daughters. Biblical names often indicate the person's attributes, and so Job's daughters are understood to be quite special.

Based on Job 42:14, note the daughter's name next to the meaning of her name:

1st daughter: ___________________________________ - meaning turtledove, which referred to graceful birds, plants and precious stones , and that which is warm, affectionate.

2nd daughter: ______________________________________ - meaning aromatic plant, cassia (cinnamon), an aromatic herb of a very fragrant smell. The agreeableness or pleasantness of the perfume was the reason why the name was chosen to be given to a daughter.

3rd daughter:____ - meaning horn of eye paint, the principal cosmetic of female beauty, a name that indicated great beauty.

He called the first Jemimah, because she was as fair as the day; the second Ketsiah, because she was as precious as cassia; the third Keren-happuch, because her face was as splendid as the emerald.[114]

These daughters were beautiful and quite a catch for whoever might marry them! They had an inheritance just like their brothers, which was very unusual. Job's gift of inheritance to his daughters shows his great wealth and his fairness to all.

The book of Job closes by mentioning two more specific blessings he enjoyed. What are they, according to Job 42:16?

Some say that Job may have been between 60 and 70 years old when his suffering began. We don't know how long it lasted, but just adding 140 years of life to 60 or 70 would give him at least around 200 years of life. One ancient text of Job says that he lived to be 240 years old.[115] That's a long life! And since grandparents love their grandchildren and love to brag about how many they have, I expect Job had a good time with four generations of little ones!

The last description of Job is one of honor and blessing. What does Job 42:17 say?

This was also said about a few other God-fearing men.

- Then Abraham breathed his last and died at a good old age, an old man who had lived a full life. He joined his ancestors. **Genesis 25:8** NET
- And Isaac breathed his last, and he died and was gathered to his people, old and full of days. And his sons Esau and Jacob buried him. **Genesis 35:29** ESV
- David died at a good old age, full of days, riches, and honor, and his son Solomon became king in his place.**1 Chronicles 29:28** HCSB
- And the priest Jehoiada died when he was old and full of days; he was 130 years old at his death. He was buried in the city of David with the kings because he had done what was good in Israel with respect to God and His temple. **2 Chronicles 24:15-16** HCSB

Job—just a man, from Uz, who feared the Lord and turned from evil. Job—the greatest of all the men of the east. Job—a man who suffered in a similar way to Jesus. Job—a man who humbled himself before the Lord.

And the Lord blessed Job. Before his suffering. During his suffering. After his suffering. And perhaps the greatest blessing of all is that Job's life has been a testimony to the wisdom, love, and sovereignty of God ever since his life on earth; and it will also stand as evidence for all eternity. The ultimate "eulogy" over Job's life is the inspired Scripture we know as the Book of Job. Perhaps his family and friends stood by his grave and quoted his words of faith: The Lord gives and the Lord takes away. Blessed be the Name of the Lord.

Lesson 40 ∾ THE BOOK OF JOB

REMEMBERING AND REFLECTING

Before we say goodbye to Job, let's review some of the profound truths that we have hopefully come to understand a little better. The Book of Job is full of intricate details, but the overall message is so important to absorb.

Please consider Job's life before, during, and after his suffering.
Why was Job blessed before his suffering? (Job 1:1,10; Job 29:1-5)

Did Job worship God because of His blessings? (Job 1)

Why was Job chosen to suffer? (Job 1—2)

During his suffering, did Job ever demand that God restore His blessings?

What do you think Job's perspective about God's blessing on his life would have been after his suffering and encounter with God?

I don't think Job would have taken any blessings for granted. He would have remembered what he learned from the Lord, that He can do anything He wants. No purpose of His can be thwarted. If the Lord wanted to choose Job to suffer again, He could.

A very important concept for us to grasp from the book of Job is that the Lord can do whatever He wants in our lives. Just because God gave Job earthly blessings after his suffering does not mean that He will act the same way in our lives. Godly couples who experience infertility may never have a child of their own. Christians who are victims of natural disasters may never have their treasured family heirlooms restored to them. Faithful followers of Jesus may be diagnosed with life-changing diseases or become handicapped, deaf, or blind. You probably know stories of dear missionaries whose family members died on the mission field due to attacks, persecutions, or health complications.

As I mentioned in the previous lesson, there is more to life than a blissful mortal existence on planet Earth.

Based on all that we've studied, what was God's purpose in allowing Job's suffering?

And now, in conclusion, please read through these verses from Job. He expressed that he wanted his words to be engraved in stone forever. May they be written on our hearts eternally. Mark your favorites and note why it is meaningful to you.

NKJ **Job 1:1** There was a man in the land of Uz whose name was Job, and that man was blameless and upright, one who feared God and turned away from evil.

Job 1:8 And the Lord said to Satan, "Have you considered my servant Job, that there is none like him on the earth, a blameless and upright man, who fears God and turns away from evil?"

Job 1:12 And the Lord said to Satan, "Behold, all that he has is in your hand. Only against him do not stretch out your hand." So Satan went out from the presence of the Lord.

Job 1:20 Then Job arose and tore his robe and shaved his head and fell on the ground and worshipped.

Job 1:21 And he said, "Naked I came from my mother's womb, and naked shall I return. The LORD gave, and the LORD has taken away; blessed be the name of the LORD."

Job 2:9-10 Then his wife said to him, "Do you still hold fast to your integrity? Curse God and die!" But he said to her, "You speak as one of the foolish women would speak. Shall we receive good from God, and shall we not receive evil?" In all of this Job did not sin with his lips.

Job 3:23-24 Why is light given to a man whose way is hidden, whom God has hedged in? For my sighing comes instead of my bread, and my groanings are poured out like water.

Job 9:2 Truly I know that it is so: But how can a man be in the right before God?

Job 9:10 (The Lord), who does great things beyond searching out, and marvelous things beyond number.

Job 12:7-10 But ask the beasts, and they will teach you; the birds of the heavens, and they will tell you; or the bushes of the earth, and they will teach you; and the fish of the sea will declare to you. Who among all these does not know that the hand of the LORD has done this? In his hand is the life of every living thing and the breath of all mankind.

Job 12:13 With God are wisdom and might; He has counsel and understanding.

Job 13:15 Though He slay me, I will hope in Him.

Job 16:19-21 Even now, behold, my witness is in heaven, and He who testifies for me is on high. My friends scorn me; my eye pours out tears to God, that He would argue the case of a man with God, as a son of man does with his neighbor.

Job 19:25 For I know that my Redeemer lives, and at the last He will stand upon the earth.

Job 23:10 But He knows the way that I take; when He has tried me, I shall come out as gold.

Job 23:13-14 But He is unchangeable, and who can turn Him back? What He desires, that He does. For He will complete what He appoints for me, and many such things are in His mind.

Job 27:3-4 As long as my breath is in me, and the Spirit of God is in my nostrils, my lips will not speak falsehood, and my tongue will not utter deceit.

Job 28:12-13 But where shall wisdom be found? And where is the place of understanding? Man does not know its worth, and it is not found in the land of the living.

Job 28:28 And He said to man, "Behold, the fear of the Lord, that is wisdom, and to turn away from evil is understanding."

Job 38:1-4 Then the LORD answered Job out of the whirlwind and said: "Who is this that darkens counsel by words without knowledge? Dress for action like a man; I will question you, and you make it known to me. Where were you when I laid the foundation of the earth? Tell me, if you have understanding."

Job 38:36 Who has put wisdom in the inward parts or given understanding to the mind?

Job 40:2 Shall a faultfinder contend with the Almighty? He who argues with God, let him answer it.

Job 40:3-5 Then Job answered the LORD and said, "Behold, I am of small account; what shall I answer you? I lay my hand on my mouth. I have spoken once, and I will not answer; twice, but I will proceed no further."

Job 40:6-9 Then the LORD answered Job out of the whirlwind and said: "Dress for action like a man; I will question you, and you make it known to me. Will you even put Me in the wrong? Will you condemn Me that you may be in the right? Have you an arm like God, and can you thunder with a voice like His?"

Job 42:2, 5-6 I know that You can do all things, and that no purpose of Yours can be thwarted. I had heard of You by the hearing of the ear, but now my eye sees You, therefore I despise myself, and repent in dust and ashes.

Job 42:9 So Eliphaz the Temanite and Bildad the Shuhite and Zophar the Naamathite went and did what the LORD had told them, and the LORD accepted Job's prayer.

Job 42:10 And the LORD restored the fortunes of Job, when he had prayed for his friends. And the LORD gave Job twice as much as he had before.

Job 42:12 And the LORD blessed the latter days of Job more than his beginning.

Thank You Lord for Your blessing of ____

____

Blessed be the Name of the Lord.

ENDNOTES

1. Warren Wiersbe. *Be Patient.* Job. David C. Cook, Colorado Springs, 1991, 17.
2. Barnes Commentary, e-sword.net.
3. Wiersbe, *Be Patient,* 138-140.
4. J. Vernon McGee, *Job*. Thomas Nelson Publishers, Nashville, 1991,16.
5. Elmer B. Smick, "1. Satan's accusations of Job (1:6-12)" In *The Expositor's Bible Commentary,* Volume 4, Grand Rapids: Zondervan Publishing House, 1988.
6. Charles R. Swindoll, *Job.* The W Publishing Group, Nashville, 2004, 24.
7. Swindoll, 24.
8. David J. A. Clines, *Job.* Word Biblical Commentary, Volume 18, Nashville, Thomas Nelson Publishers, 2006, 45.
9. Swindoll, 45.
10. Smick, Elmer B. "4. Job's integrity in personal suffering (2:7-10)" In *The Expositor's Bible Commentary*: Volume 4. 885. Grand Rapids: Zondervan Publishing House, 1988.
11. Steven J. Lawson, *Job.* Holman Old Testament Commentary, B & H Publishing Group, Nashville, 2004,19.
12. Swindoll, 39.
13. Clines, 87.
14. Wiersbe, 26.
15. Lawson, 41.
16. "You've God a Friend in Me." Written by Randy Newman, Published by Lyrics, Walt Disney Music Publishing Company
17. Wiersbe, 35.
18. Swindoll, 85.
19. Swindoll, 85.
20. Wiersbe, 41.
21. John Gill, Job 8:1-2 in *John Gill's Exposition of the Entire Bible,* www.e-sword.net
22. Smick, Elmer B. "3. Bildad (8:1-22)" In *The Expositor's Bible Commentary*: Volume 4. 905. Grand Rapids: Zondervan Publishing House, 1988.
23. Clines, 207.
24. Clines, 203.
25. Lawson, 86.
26. Smick, Elmer B. "5. Zophar (11:1-20)" In *The Expositor's Bible Commentary*: Volume 4. 916. Grand Rapids: Zondervan Publishing House, 1988.
27. Smick, Elmer B. "5. Zophar (11:1-20)" In *The Expositor's Bible Commentary*: Volume 4. 917. Grand Rapids: Zondervan Publishing House, 1988.
28. McGee, 74.
29. C. S. Lewis, *The Lion, the Witch and the Wardrobe*. New York: Scholastic, 1995
30. Lawson, 104.
31. http://www.washburn.edu/academics/college-schools/arts-sciences/departments/communication/nall-speak-off/
32. Weirsbe, 62.
33. Lawson, 111.
34. Clines, 296.
35. The Jewish Study Bible, *Job 13:4,* Jewish Publication Society TANAKH translation, 1985, 1999 by the Jewish Publication Society, Oxford University Press, New York.
36. Wiersbe, 65.
37. Stephen Davey, *Job.* Wisdom Commentary Series, Charity House Publishers, Apex, NC, 2014, 150.
38. Holman Christian Study Bible, *note on Job 14:20-21.* Copyright 2010 by Holman Bible Publishers, Nashville, TN.
39. Lawson, 130.
40. NIV, Faith in Action Study Bible, eBook: Living God's Word in a Changing World. Job 15:1-35. Terry C. Muck, Contributor; Harper Collins, 2011.
41. Wiersbe, 74.
42. http://www.imdb.com/title/tt2528814/quotes
43. Matthew Henry (1706). *Job 17:4.* In *Matthew Henry Commentary on the Whole Bible (complete), Bibleworks Software.*
44. Henry, Job 2.

45. Jamieson, Robert, A.R. Fausset, David Brown, Job 16:21. *A commentary, critical and explanatory, on the whole Bible, with introduction to Old Testament literature, a pronouncing dictionary of Scripture proper names, tables of weights and measures, and an index to the entire Bible.* George H. Doran Co., New York, 1921.
46. Lawson, 152.
47. http://en.wikipedia.org/wiki/Cello_Sonata_%28Debussy%29
48. Wiersbe, 86.
49. Wiersbe, 89.
50. Wiersbe, 98.
51. Shepherd's Notes — *Job*. Duane A. Garrett, editor. B & H Publishing Group, Nashville, 1998, 47.
52. Lawson, 188.
53. http://www.abbottandcostellofanclub.com/who.html
54. Lawson, 195.
55. Smick, Elmer B. "1. Eliphaz (22:1-30)" In *The Expositor's Bible Commentary*: Volume 4. 954. Grand Rapids: Zondervan Publishing House, 1988.
56. Smick, Elmer B. "1. Eliphaz (22:1-30)" In *The Expositor's Bible Commentary*: Volume 4. 954. Grand Rapids: Zondervan Publishing House, 1988.
57. John H. Walton, *The NIV Application Commentary: Job,* p. 246. *Zondervan, Grand Rapids, MI, 2012.*
58. Swindoll, ix.
59. Smick, Elmer B. "2. Job's reply (23:1-24:25)" In *The Expositor's Bible Commentary*: Volume 4. 957. Grand Rapids: Zondervan Publishing House, 1988.
60. Barnes, Job 23:2.
61. Swindoll, 61.
62. Kelley Carroll
63. Lawson, 220.
64. Wiersbe, 125.
65. Walton, 264.
66. Smick, Elmer B. "4. Job's reply (26:1-14)" In *The Expositor's Bible Commentary*: Volume 4. 967. Grand Rapids: Zondervan Publishing House, 1988.
67. Lawson, 225.
68. Wiersbe, 126.
69. Barnes, Job 26:5-13.
70. Swindoll, 201.
71. Lawson, 234.
72. Lawson, 234.
73. Tremper Longman III, Job. *Baker Commentary on the Old Testament Wisdom and Psalms*, Baker Academic, Grand Rapids MI, 2012, 329.
74. Wiersbe, 132.
75. https://www.justsomelyrics.com/1558269/various-more-precious-than-silver-%28lynn-deshazo%29-lyrics.html
76. Shepherd's Notes, 66.
77. http://www.brainyquote.com/quotes/quotes/a/alfredlord153711.html
78. Longman, 342.
79. Swindoll, 39.
80. Shepherd's Notes, 70.
81. Holman Christian Study Bible, note on Job 31:35-37.
82. John E. Hartley, *Job*. The New International Commentary on the Old Testament, Wm. B. Eerdmans Publishing Co. Grand Rapids, MI, 1988, 429.
83. Davey, 233.
84. C. S. Lewis, *The Problem of Pain,* Harper/Collins, 1940, 91.
85. Hartley, 459.
86. McGee, 172.
87. Shepherd's Notes,80.
88. Smick, Elmer B. "6. The fourth speech (36:1-37:24)" In *The Expositor's Bible Commentary*: Volume 4. 1023. Grand Rapids: Zondervan Publishing House, 1988.
89. Walton, 370.
90. Wiersbe, 179.
91. Lawson, 329.
92. Robin Kerrod, *The Star Guide.* Macmillan USA Copyright 1993 Quarto Inc., 86.
93. Jay Apt, Michael Helfert and Justin Wilkinson, *Orbit: Nasa Astronauts Photograph the Earth.* National Geographic, 2003.

94. Marvin H. Pope , *Job.* Doubleday and Company, Inc. New York, 1965, 255.
95. Walton, 404.
96. Sarah Ficken
97. Smick, Elmer B. "2. Job's humbling (40:3-5)" In *The Expositor's Bible Commentary*: Volume 4. 1044-1045. Grand Rapids: Zondervan Publishing House, 1988.
98. Smick, Elmer B. "2. Job's humbling (40:3-5)" In *The Expositor's Bible Commentary*: Volume 4. 1044-1045. Grand Rapids: Zondervan Publishing House, 1988.
99. Davey, 298.
100. http://www.merriam-webster.com/dictionary/behemoth
101. http://creation.com/behemoth-and-leviathan. This article is based on Paul, M-J., van den Brink, G. and Bette, J.C. (Eds.), *Bijbelcommentaar Ezra – Job* [Bible commentary of Ezra–Job]; in: Studiebijbel Oude Testament [Study Bible of the Old Testament], vol. 6. Veenendaal: Centrum voor Bijbelonderzoek, the Netherlands, 2009; studiebijbel.nl, translated by Naomi Verboom.
102. http://creation.com/behemoth-and-leviathan
103. Brian Thomas, M.S. 2015. Was Leviathan Real?. *Acts & Facts*. 44 (2).
104. Davey, 303.
105. Davey, 303-304.
106. Davey, 304.
107. Holman Christian Study Bible, note on Job 42:3.
108. *Theological Wordbook of the Old Testament*, Volumes 1 & 2. R. Laird Harris, Editor. Moody Press, Chicago, 1980.
109. Lawson, 366.
110. Smick, Elmer B. "D. Job's Closing Contrition (42:1-6)" In *The Expositor's Bible Commentary*: Volume 4. 1056. Grand Rapids: Zondervan Publishing House, 1988.
111. Smick, Elmer B. "A. The Verdict (42:7-9)" In *The Expositor's Bible Commentary*: Volume 4. 1057. Grand Rapids: Zondervan Publishing House, © 1988.
112. Hartley, 539.
113. Hartley, 539.
114. *Adam Clarke's Commentary on the Whole Bible*, Job 42:14, e-sword.net.
115. *Adam Clarke's Commentary on the Whole Bible*, Job 42:16, e-sword.net.

SUGGESTED RESOURCES

Shepherd's Notes: Job. Duane A. Garrett, editor. © 1998 by B&H Publishing Group, Nashville, TN.

The Strongest Strong's Exhaustive Concordance by James Strong — available through online resources below and Google

Suggested (free) online study helps:

These include various Bible translations and links to all resources mentioned below.

studylight.org **biblestudytools.org** **blueletterbible.org**

e-sword.net (free program to download, then available offline)

The following list includes study helps that are available for free online if you are interested in pursuing more information about the Scriptures on your own. Descriptions are from e-sword.net.

Commentaries:

Robertson's Word Pictures in the New Testament

Robertson's magnum opus has a reputation as one of the best New Testament word study sets. Providing verse-by-verse commentary, it stresses meaningful and pictorial nuances implicit in the Greek but often lost in translation. And for those who do not know Greek, exegetical material and interpretive insights are directly connected with studies in the original text. All Greek words are transliterated.

Treasury of Scriptural Knowledge

This classic Bible study help gives you a concordance, chain-reference system, topical Bible and commentary all in one! Turn to any Bible passage, and you'll find chapter synopses, key word cross-references, topical references, parallel passages and illustrative notes that show how the Bible comments on itself. This really is a treasure!

Vincent's Word Studies

Marvin Vincent's Word Studies has been treasured by generations of pastors and laypeople. Commenting on the meaning, derivation, and uses of significant Greek words and idioms, Vincent helps you incorporate the riches of the New Testament in your sermons or personal study without spending hours on tedious language work!

John Gill's Exposition of the Entire Bible

Having preached in the same church as C. H. Spurgeon, John Gill is little known, but his works contain gems of information found nowhere outside of the ancient Jewish writings. John Gill presents a verse-by-verse exposition of the entire Bible.

Jamieson, Fausset and Brown Commentary
Long considered one of the best conservative commentaries on the entire Bible, the JFB Bible Commentary offers practical insight from a reformed evangelical perspective. The comments are an insightful balance between learning and devotion, with an emphasis on allowing the text to speak for itself.

Keil & Delitzsch Commentary on the Old Testament
This commentary is a classic in conservative biblical scholarship! Beginning with the nature and format of the Old Testament, this evangelical commentary examines historical and literary aspects of the text, as well as grammatical and philological issues. Hebrew words and grammar are used, but usually in content, so you can follow the train of thought.

Dictionaries:

Easton's Bible Dictionary
Easton's Bible Dictionary provides informative explanations of histories, people and customs of the Bible. An excellent and readily understandable source of information for the student and layperson. This dictionary is one of Matthew George Easton's most significant literary achievements.

International Standard Bible Encyclopedia
This authoritative reference dictionary explains every significant word in the Bible and Apocrypha! Learn about archaeological discoveries, the language and literature of Bible lands, customs, family life, occupations, and the historical and religious environments of Bible people.

Smith's Bible Dictionary
A classic reference, this comprehensive Bible dictionary gives you thousands of easy-to-understand definitions, verse references and provides a wealth of basic background information that you'll find indispensable as you read the Bible.

Thayer's Greek Definitions
For over a century, Joseph Henry Thayer's Greek-English Lexicon of the New Testament has been lauded as one of the finest available! Based on the acclaimed German lexicon by C.L.W. Grimm, Thayer's work adds comprehensive extra-biblical citations and etymological information, expanded references to other works, increased analysis of textual variations, and discussion of New Testament synonyms. An invaluable resource for students of New Testament Greek!

Noah Webster's Dictionary of American English
Noah Webster once wrote, "Education is useless without the Bible." That's why his first dictionary is the only one available today that defines every word in the original language and its biblical usage. Compare Webster's definitions of words like "marriage" and "education" with those found in modern dictionaries, and see the difference for yourself!

Prayer Requests and Blessings

Today's Date:
My personal request:

Confidential requests from my friends:

Bless the LORD, O my soul, And forget not all His benefits.
Psalm 103:2 [NKJ]

Prayer Requests and Blessings

Today's Date:
My personal request:

Confidential requests from my friends:

I will sing to the Lord, because He has dealt bountifully with me
Psalm 13:6 NKJV

Today's Date:
My personal request:

Confidential requests from my friends:

Oh, taste and see that the Lord is good: blessed is the man who trusts in Him!
Psalm 34:8 NKJV

Prayer Requests and Blessings

Today's Date:
My personal request:

Confidential requests from my friends:

Dear friend, I pray that you may enjoy good health and that all may go well with you, even as your soul is getting along well.
3 John 1:2 NIV

Prayer Requests and Blessings

Today's Date:
My personal request:

Confidential requests from my friends:

The Lord bless you and keep you; The Lord make His face shine upon you, and be gracious to you; The Lord lift up His countenance upon you and give you peace.
Numbers 6:24-26 NKJV

Today's Date:
My personal request:

Confidential requests from my friends:

The Lord God is a sun and shield; The Lord will give grace and glory; No good thing will He withhold from those who walk uprightly.
Psalm 84:11 NKJV

Prayer Requests and Blessings

Today's Date:
My personal request:

Confidential requests from my friends:

Behold, I am the Lord, the God of all flesh, is there anything too hard for me?
Jeremiah 32:27 NKJV

Prayer Requests and Blessings

Today's Date:
My personal request:

Confidential requests from my friends:

Then you will call upon Me and come and pray to Me, and I will listen to you.
Jeremiah 29:12 (BOA)

Prayer Requests and Blessings

Today's Date:
My personal request:

Confidential requests from my friends:

As I was with Moses, so I will be with you; I will never leave you or forsake you.
Joshua 1:5 NIV

Today's Date:
My personal request:

Confidential requests from my friends:

Trust in the Lord with all your heart and lean not on your own understanding; in all your ways acknowledge Him, and He will make your paths straight.
Proverbs 3:5-6 NIV

Prayer Requests and Blessings

Today's Date:
My personal request:

Confidential requests from my friends:

My God shall supply all your need according to His riches in glory by Christ Jesus.
Philippians 4:19 KJV

Prayer Requests and Blessings

Today's Date:
My personal request:

Confidential requests from my friends:

The God of Israel Himself gives strength and power to the people.
Psalm 68:35

Prayer Requests and Blessings

Today's Date:
My personal request:

Confidential requests from my friends:

Always keep on praying for all the saints.
Ephesians 6:18 NIV

Prayer Requests and Blessings

Today's Date:
My personal request:

Confidential requests from my friends:

I call to God, and the Lord saves me. Evening, morning and noon
I cry out in distress, and He hears my voice.
Psalm 55:16-17 NIV

Prayer Requests and Blessings

Today's Date:
My personal request:

Confidential requests from my friends:

You help us by your prayers.
2 Corinthians 1:11 NIV

Prayer Requests and Blessings

Today's Date:
My personal request:

Confidential requests from my friends:

If you abide in Me, and My words abide in you,
ask whatever you wish, and it shall be done for you.
John 15:7 NASB

Prayer Requests and Blessings

Today's Date:
My personal request:

Confidential requests from my friends:

Let us therefore come boldly to the throne of grace,
that we may obtain mercy and find grace to help in time of need.
Hebrews 4:16

Prayer Requests and Blessings

Today's Date:
My personal request:

Confidential requests from my friends:

Be joyful always; pray continually; give thanks in all circumstances,
for this is God's will for you in Christ Jesus.
1 Thessalonians 5:16-18 NIV

Prayer Requests and Blessings

Today's Date:
My personal request:

Confidential requests from my friends:

...Far be it from me that I should sin against You, O Lord, by ceasing to pray for others.[6]
1 Samuel 12:23

Prayer Requests and Blessings

Today's Date:
My personal request:

Confidential requests from my friends:

Do not be anxious about anything, but in everything, by prayer and petition, with thanksgiving, present your requests to God.
Philippians 4:6 NIV

Prayer Requests and Blessings

Today's Date:
My personal request:

Confidential requests from my friends:

With God are wisdom and might; He has counsel and understanding.
Job 12:13 HCSB

Prayer Requests and Blessings

Today's Date:
My personal request:

Confidential requests from my friends:

And the LORD accepted Job's prayer.
Job 42:9 HCSB

Notes

Notes

Notes

Notes

Notes

Notes

OTHER STUDIES BY ELIZABETH BAGWELL FICKEN

Come Let Us Worship: An in-depth Bible study of Psalms

The Psalms contain many of our most well-known Scriptures, offering comfort and expressing the emotions of our souls. They challenge us to godly living, always trusting the Lord. What a beautiful arrangement of poems, prayers, and praises God has given us! From Psalm 1 to Psalm 150, you'll study selected psalms in the order of their placement in the Scriptures.

That You May Know the Lord: An in-depth Bible study of Ezekiel

Don't miss this great book! As you study this intriguing prophecy, you will be humbled by the holiness, sovereignty and glory of God; you will be challenged to examine your own lives as you see the sin of the Israelites; you will be inspired as you see the power of the Holy Spirit; and you will be excited as you anticipate wonderful promises to be fulfilled by the Lord.

Justice and Mercy — The Character of God, the Messiah, and the Kingdom: An in-depth Bible study of Micah

Who is like God? The prophet Micah tells us! This short book of prophecy declares God's judgment against injustice which will prompt us to examine how we live our lives and treat others. It also declares God's overwhelming mercy to forgive sins. And it unveils the Lord's extraordinary plans for Israel during the Millennial Kingdom when Jesus Christ reigns supreme.

Follow Me: An in-depth Bible study of the Gospel of Matthew

This study will challenge you to a more passionate commitment to Jesus. Learn from Matthew's eye-witness perspective, his proofs from Old Testament scriptures, and his presentation of Jesus' five sermons, just who Jesus is, what He did, and what He said. Matthew's life was drastically changed from his encounter with Jesus—yours will be too.

Believe in Me — The Death and Resurrection of Jesus Christ: an in-depth study of Luke 22-24

Experience an eye-opening, gut-wrenching, faith-strengthening study of Luke's carefully researched account. You'll learn that Judas the traitor was influenced by Satan. That the disciples abandoned Jesus. That powerful people testified to Jesus' innocence. That Jesus was crucified and declared dead.... And that He rose from the dead! Jesus offers freedom from sin, a relationship with His holy Father, and an eternal life of joy.

Abide in Me — Devotion and Dependence on Jesus Christ: an in-depth study of John 14-16

Can you imagine Jesus' burden for His disciples right before His death? Learn how Jesus prepared His disciples for life after His death, resurrection, and ascension. You'll understand His incredible promise that the Father would send the Holy Spirit and you'll grasp, as the disciples did, that you cannot do anything on your own, but must be dependent on Jesus, through His Holy Spirit, to do what He has commanded. And that is – to bear much fruit.

Immeasurably More!: An in-depth Bible study of Ephesians

Do you want your walk with Christ to be more intimate, more faithful, and more obedient? God is able to do immeasurably more than you can imagine through His power in your life! This exciting study will help you understand the never-ending blessings of salvation and the extraordinary potential you have to live a victorious and faithful Christian life.

Letters to the Thessalonians — Encouragement for living in the End Times: An in-depth Bible study of 1st and 2nd Thessalonians

These letters are about faith, hope and love; holiness, prayer, and perseverance; the will of God and the glorious return of Christ. And so much more! Almost every major doctrine of our faith is covered in these personal writings from the apostle Paul. Join me as we read someone else's mail. I'm sure you'll find a few things that you will think were written just to you!

Hold Fast to Jesus: An in-depth Bible study of Hebrews

In this study of the personal, passionate letter of exhortation to "go on to maturity," we'll consider deep doctrines including the New Covenant and atonement. We'll be warned not to drift away from our great salvation. We'll be encouraged to persevere through suffering as the great heroes of the faith did. We'll see that Jesus is our great High Priest who has provided what no other priest ever could. Let us fix our eyes on Jesus and hold fast to Him.

From the Author:

Thank you for studying the Bible with me! If you have enjoyed reading this book, please share a brief review on Amazon or on social media. You can help other readers decide whether to read the book too, and you can help spread the word of God!

Blessings, *Elizabeth*

Find her! elizabethficken.com or      

Thank you for studying God's word with me!

It's been such a delight and privilege and plenty of hard work
to write the Bible studies described on the previous pages.

Each is available on Amazon and at The Shepherd's Church bookstore.

Use the workbooks for:

Individual Bible study
Small group Bible study
Church classes
Homeschooling

Visit elizabethficken.com for more resources

Free Videos:
30-45 minute lectures which supplement workbook lessons,
including handouts and PowerPoint presentations

Free leader's guides:
audio discussions of how to lead each workbook lesson

Find me on your favorite podcast apps:
In-depth Bible Study with Elizabeth Ficken

Find my lectures on YouTube:
In-depth Bible Studies
@elizabethficken